SCOTT SANDERS
PICTURE
DESIGNING THE NEW AMERICAN FAMILY HOME
PERFECT

PUBLISHER / EDITORIAL DIRECTOR: SUZANNE SLESIN
DESIGN: STAFFORD CLIFF
MANAGING EDITOR: JANE K. CREECH
PRODUCTION: DOMINICK J. SANTISE JR.
TEXT: JEN RENZI
COPY EDITOR: ELIZABETH GALL

NEW PHOTOGRAPHS BY MICHEL ARNAUD
POINTED LEAF PRESS, LLC.

Introduction
Welcome Home

When it comes to historical inspirations, interior designers are typically either slavish or subversive. The scholarly types will read decorative-arts tomes and take trips to Versailles in an effort to re-create a Louis XIV period look. Those taking an irreverent stance, meanwhile, mix eras and genres with a knowing wink—rococo next to raj, Deco next to Directoire. Within this context, New York designer Scott Sanders is his own person: His spaces neither kowtow to nor send up the past. They are paeans to earlier times, inspired by contemporary lifestyles and cultural references—not dusty history books. His interiors offer up a whiff of nostalgia and even revisionism, but not of irony.

Scott's sense of history is suggestive rather than literal. In search of a good paint color for an eighteenth-century scheme, he doesn't head to Colonial Williamsburg to study historic palettes; he opens his desk drawer and pulls out a box of French blue Smythson of Bond Street stationery. He loves the cast of characters that distinguish nineteenth-century interiors: carved-wood English hall chairs, Shaker benches, wrought-iron chandeliers, and braided area rugs. But his furniture plans are more likely to be inspired by the set of *I Love Lucy* than by the writings of Elsie de Wolfe. You can feel it when you walk through his interiors: a mix of antique and classic furnishings makes the decor feel familiar and comfortable—not fussy.

Scott's design sense is not self-seriousness, and neither is he. Indeed, no one whose decorating tool kit includes inflatable lobsters and 1980s LP covers can be considered highfalutin. What's immediately apparent about Scott is his sense of lighthearted playfulness. When dropping by his client's all-blue house, he will wear a blue shirt, blue jeans, and a pair of blue Converse sneakers. He pokes fun at his own obsessions while remaining loyal to them: stripes, wing chairs, and certain furnishings he uses in almost every project. (The Scott Sanders version of *Where's Waldo?* would be *Where's the John Rosselli Hall Console?*) He is quick to laugh but not to lecture; his conversations are sprinkled with pop-cultural references and childhood anecdotes rather than the names of obscure furniture makers and architects. His spaces are as warm, relatable, and unintimidating as the designer himself.

Since founding Scott Sanders LLC in 2000, he has built a portfolio of projects that meld his two influences: an American vernacular of clean-lined antiques coupled with the unfussy classicism of Ralph Lauren, whose in-house interior design department he ran before going solo. Scott's own relationship to history is in the Ralph Lauren vein. He creates spaces that capture the joy of home—whether the actual one we grew up in or an idealized version thereof. "So many of my young clients request Colonial-style homes, not because they have an actual connection to it—they may have grown up in a modernist box—but because to them it symbolizes family," Scott says.

Such clients include Dan and Samantha Anderson, a young couple who share Scott's aesthetic sensibility. The Andersons came across one of Scott's projects in a shelter magazine and were so moved that they immediately called his office—on a Saturday afternoon in the summer—and left an enthusiastic message. "I think the phrase 'This is awesome!' was used," Scott says, laughing. The Andersons had just begun designing a new house—or, rather, a *new-old* house: a nine-thousand-square-foot stone and clapboard Pennsylvania Dutch–style Colonial located on three-plus acres in rural New Jersey. The Andersons were determined to build a house that had integrity and heart.

Although furnishings were installed in a fast-and-furious five days, the project actually took much longer to complete: four years. It was a testament to quality construction—a process that cannot be rushed—and Scott's meticulous, all-encompassing approach to interior decoration. Although he will, if asked, build a new decor around a client's existing pieces, Scott loves a clean slate, picking out everything from new silverware to bathroom towels—and even books, which he purchases by the foot according to a particular color or theme. He loves to curate collections of art or accessories—anything from equestrian-themed drawings to vintage pottery—that clients can continue to build over time.

Designing the Anderson house became the culmination of every project Scott had worked on previously—from the Hampton Designer Showhouse to a Miami hotel—as well as memories of his own upbringing. Even so, Scott's small-town childhood is his greatest source of inspiration. Born and raised in Piqua, Ohio, the designer's childhood was conventionally idyllic: riding bikes around leafy neighborhoods, visiting Grandma's house nearby, taking family trips to the Henry Ford Museum's Greenfield Village. His dad and grandfather were residential developers, building subdivisions with streets named after his cousins and aunts, who all lived in the same town. The traditional two-story Colonials—with four bedrooms, two and a half bathrooms, and a two-car garage—were the prototypical suburban nuclear-family dream. All signs pointed to his growing up to become a designer: He constantly redecorated his shag-carpeted bedroom, hoarded files of tear sheets from his mother's copies of *Better Homes and Gardens,* and drew floor plans based on his favorite seventies sitcoms, as well as houses of his own imagination. "I was always scrambling for paper—whatever I could find to draw on!" Scott says.

While the male members of the family nursed Scott's appetite for architecture, the women honed his decorative sense. He has strong memories of his paternal grandmother's 1920s neo-Colonial home decorated with a Duncan Phyfe dining set, a red glass backsplash in the kitchen, and a replica of an ice cream parlor in the basement. Scott's other grandmother, Mimi, moved every few years, from a 1950s saltbox to an early-sixties modernist gem and then to a Spanish colonial. "She had what my mom called Gypsy feet," Scott says. "Mimi constantly redecorated, but she mostly reused and reworked her existing furniture by reupholstering and moving things around. She made creative use of what she had; that Midwestern resourcefulness informs my work." And her love of bold hues inspires Scott's own color sense. "Her fire-engine red shag carpeting and floral drapes are forever imprinted in my brain."

So is the sense of warmth and togetherness he experienced growing up, and that informs every design choice he makes to this day. "Everyone in my extended family—all of whom lived nearby—inhabited spaces that were beautifully and tastefully appointed with integrity and realness," Scott says. "But they were not about the design per se; they were about creating comfortable backdrops for family time together." Now, there's a sentiment that is indeed timeless. ⒮

OPPOSITE With one foot resting on an Eames chair, Scott relaxes in his khaki-and-blue office in New York's Flatiron district. Behind him hangs a site plan of the Anderson house.

Chapter One
A Very Young Designer

I was raised in the middle of the country—Piqua, Ohio, population 19,000—by a design-centric family. Everyone had a strong aesthetic: My father and grandfather were residential developers, my mother had a way with furniture and fabrics, and both my grandmothers were amazing amateur decorators. As a result, I developed a heightened awareness of my surroundings, and much of my childhood was spent drawing pictures of houses. Looking back, I'm amazed at the level of detail I captured: floor plans that included the placement of windows, lighting, plants, and "phones," which I had designated with a little "p." One house even had an art studio with a stack of canvases by a wall. When I wasn't drawing, I built models and decorated them with carpet and tile samples I had begged my parents for. White Lego furniture that I designed, built, and placed on light blue carpeting was my signature statement.

Around the age of twelve, I stopped drawing. I still had creative outlets—fabricating theater sets, writing, and editing the school newspaper—but my design impulse receded for a few years. Working on the high school yearbook, *The Piquonian,* was what ultimately rebooted my visual interests. As editor in chief my senior year, I oversaw everything from the layouts to the typefaces. The experience must have flicked on a switch, because I recently found floor plans sketched on the graph paper we used for the yearbook page templates. I've been designing dream homes ever since. But now I get to build them. ⑤

LEFT One of Scott's early crayon drawings, made when he was six, demonstrates that from a very young age he was obsessed with houses.

self-portrait
1-1969

OPPOSITE Recently, in his parents' attic in Ohio, Scott came across a box filled with childhood drawings he and his older sister had made. Labeled "Early Works by Scott and Sharon," the stash revealed that he had favored architecture over people. He found only a few self-portraits among the lot—including this one, done when he was about six years old.

RIGHT Scott's second-grade class photograph shows his signature glasses and blond curls. "Growing up as a creative child in a very small town—Piqua, Ohio—I was somewhat of a misfit, which is probably why I spent so much time drawing," he says.

TINY TOTS

Joey Aber · Karla Hahn · Tammie Spain · Julie Newnam · Toddie Bruner · Dianna Stengel · Curtie South · Tammy Cecil

Dougie Kinsella · Missi Ferree · Randy Petty · Kathy Kruse · Donnie Widney · Nikki Adams · Scotty Sanders · Cynthia Lester

Mikey Heckerman · Kimmy McMaken · Susie Davis · Lisa Ventura · Terry Mayo · Joycie Whiteford · Danny McMillan · Nancy Stahl

Annie Siegel · Jaynie Anderson · Gina Keels · Jamie Baker · Tammy Neth · Bonny Elifritz · Stevie and Kathy Kappeler · Connie Francis

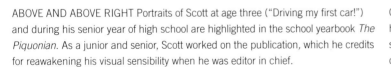

Laurie Shaffer · Martie Ary · Thaddie Good · Lisa Montgomery · Terri Chronerberry · Lynn Vonaschen · Krissy Fair · Mikey Fair

Mikey Stang · Rhonda Sorrell · Molly Mechling · Kentie Wise · Lisa Kazer · Tammy Millhoff · Kathy Smith · Jimmy Jennings

Tracey Honeyeutt · Donna Apple · Kimmy DeBrosse · Candy Huffman · Lois Bates · Gina Ross · Ruthie Argabright · Cathy Dunn

Debbie Felver · Brenda Livesay · Glennie Ash · Braddie Havenar · Tweetie, Tommy and Scotty at Nursery School · Marty and Kevin were chums

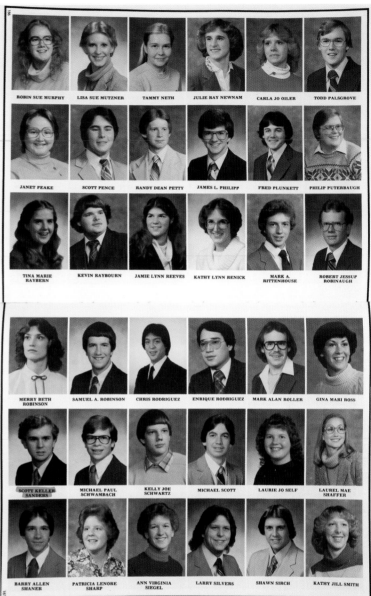

ROBIN SUE MURPHY · LISA SUE MUTZNER · TAMMY NETH · JULIE RAY NEWNAM · CARLA JO OILER · TODD PALSGROVE

JANET PEAKE · SCOTT PENCE · RANDY DEAN PETTY · JAMES L. PHILIPP · FRED PLUNKETT · PHILIP PUTERBAUGH

TINA MARIE RAYBERN · KEVIN RAYBOURN · JAMIE LYNN REEVES · KATHY LYNN RENICK · MARK A. RITTENHOUSE · ROBERT JESSUP ROBINAUGH

MERRY BETH ROBINSON · SAMUEL A. ROBINSON · CHRIS RODRIGUEZ · ENRIQUE RODRIGUEZ · MARK ALAN ROLLER · GINA MARI ROSS

SCOTT KELLER SANDERS · MICHAEL PAUL SCHWAMBACH · KELLY JOE SCHWARTZ · MICHAEL SCOTT · LAURIE JO SELF · LAUREL MAE SHAFFER

BARRY ALLEN SHANER · PATRICIA LENORE SHARP · ANN VIRGINIA SIEGEL · LARRY SILVERS · SHAWN SIRCH · KATHY JILL SMITH

ABOVE AND ABOVE RIGHT Portraits of Scott at age three ("Driving my first car!") and during his senior year of high school are highlighted in the school yearbook *The Piquonian*. As a junior and senior, Scott worked on the publication, which he credits for reawakening his visual sensibility when he was editor in chief.

OPPOSITE The designer relaxes in the double-height living room of a client's beach house in Bridgehampton, New York. "The funny thing about this photograph," he says, "is that I look exactly like I did in the self-portrait I drew when I was six—same curly hair and preppy clothes."

RIGHT Many of Scott's childhood drawings were inspired by construction sites he explored with his father and grandfather. Here, a circular driveway spiraling around a tree leads to a two-story house with a colonnaded front porch and double chimneys.

BELOW Furniture placement was often inspired by the set design of houses in favorite television sitcoms like *The Partridge Family*. His drawings had rather adult indulgences such as wine cellars, music rooms, and double-sided fireplaces—as well as more kid-friendly features like foosball tables and pinball machines.

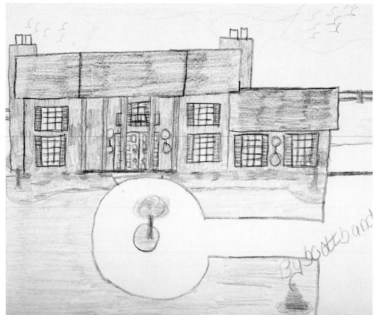

RIGHT Houses were rendered in exacting detail, down to the window treatments, roof shingles, and hanging plants. "My grandfather often solicited my opinion on the exterior of the houses he built, so I became very sensitive to the design of facades," Scott says.

BELOW Sketching plans for entire housing developments was one of Scott's favorite activities. His fantasy versions of suburban subdivisions often included houses, trees, pools, and even tennis courts.

OVERLEAF Scott loved drawing house facades with a Bic ballpoint pen and colored pencils. The renderings often featured elements from nearby homes, such as a sundeck above the garage (bottom row, third from left). "That detail came from Mrs. Wise's house. She lived down the street from my grandmother, Thelma Sanders," says Scott. But the brick walkways and leaded-glass windows were not part of his hometown vernacular. These were probably inspired by designs he saw in magazines or at the Home-a-Rama, a trade show in Ohio where developers promoted their new plans. Whether English Tudor or mid-century modern, Scott's houses featured hanging plants, elaborate front yard landscaping, and curtained windows with dangling tiebacks.

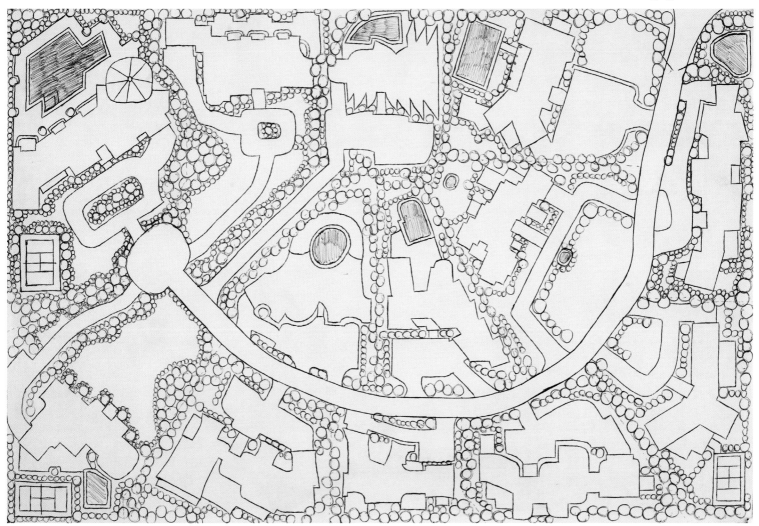

English Tudor

Pool and guesthouse

French provincial

Brick walkway

Manicured trees

Mansard roof

16

Classic two-story

Cool, modern ranch

Dramatic rooflines

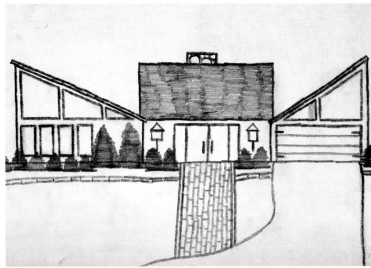
Sprawling contemporary

Colonial with sundeck

Landscaped mid-century

PREVIOUS PAGES A love of modern architecture is evident in Scott's drawing of an unusual hilltop home distinguished by broad expanses of glass and a severely angled roofline. "Piqua, Ohio, was quite traditional, so modern homes really stood out," Scott says. He was fascinated by one down the street that had full-height windows and a low-slung roof. "People would say under their breath, 'Oh, there's a *modern* house.' It was like a dirty word, which, of course, made it more intriguing."

LEFT A watercolor depicts the first house the Sanders family lived in that was built by Scott's grandfather Bill McVety and was located in Park Ridge, one of the subdivisions he developed.

BELOW LEFT Bill and his wife, who was called Mimi by her family, also built a Spanish-themed home, named Cortega, in Piqua in the 1970s. Scott counts his rose-tinted memories of this home as his biggest influence.

OPPOSITE The living room of Cortega featured fire-engine red shag carpeting and coordinating fabrics. Mimi's deft mix of different wood finishes—such as a white French provincial bookcase and antique ebonized Hitchcock chairs—has become Scott's trademark, too. Matching quilted bedspreads are paired with Early American headboards in a guest room. Mimi juxtaposed a dark-stained Early American hutch with a French provincial dining set. Yellow wrought-iron furniture brightened the breakfast area.

OVERLEAF Scott's other grandfather, Keller Sanders, owned Sanders Dairy, Milk, and Ice Cream. Although his father closed the business when Scott was very young, he grew up playing in the basement of his grandmother's Colonial-style home, which housed a replica of the 1950s ice cream store complete with checkerboard-tiled floor, red vinyl banquettes, a Coca-Cola cooler, a baby grand piano, and a drum set.

A Colonial house has blue-painted clapboard siding.

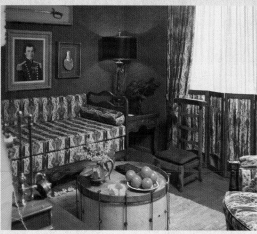

The drum table is the same one that was once in his family's rumpus room.

Walls, draperies, and furnishings covered in matching fabric was a never-forgotten decorating trick.

When Scott recently visited his parents in Ohio, he found a file of pages he had torn from decorating magazines as a kid. "These clippings must be etched in my subconscious, because this is *exactly* how I design today," he says. "I was clearly attached to these images without realizing it."

A utility room with a Masonite-pegboard wall painted bright blue was a memorable detail.

Colorful countertops were another favorite detail, though clients now often shy away from them.

Versions of this breakfast room's wrought-iron chandelier are still on the designer's agenda.

Yellow-and-green fabric accented by a black chair was a memorable combination.

A kitchen treated to a lively wallpaper pattern caught the young designer's eye.

The wing chair and double-tiered chandelier in this dark, clubby den are elements that would resurface years later.

A 1970s glossary of nineteenth-century antiques would influence Scott's later repertoire.

From the same source, a primer on Pennsylvania Dutch Colonial furniture illustrates a favorite turned-wood armchair and trestle table.

"I've always liked ancestral portraits—whether they are really of one's relatives or not," Scott says.

A den with a wing chair and plushly upholstered club chair flanking a fireplace and built-in bookcase prefigures Scott's family-room designs.

A wing chair upholstered in a blue-and-white toile de Jouy was memorable.

Chapter Two
Building a Career

My aesthetic—as well as my professional career—is the by-product of two major influences: my all-American childhood, and the decade spent working at Ralph Lauren prior to launching my own firm in 2000. I started with Ralph Lauren in 1990, as a manager of their retail shop in Stamford, Connecticut. Eight years later, I was the first interior designer at the Madison Avenue flagship store in New York, working on outside clients' homes. Ralph Lauren is a wonderfully encompassing world, and I really lived the brand. The first year I worked there, I think I wore cashmere sweaters and crocodile shoes every single day! It was sensorial overload, just like my childhood.

Ralph Lauren shaped my decorating worldview by showing me how even the smallest detail could reflect and communicate a larger design vision. The job also fine-tuned my sensitivity to fabrics by teaching me how to mix classic patterns and colors to create cohesion. But the best thing was that each home collection was completely different from the previous one: rustic one season, and refined the next. I loved that I could use current pieces to design a crazy Southwestern cowboy pad and then move on to an English gentleman's library. The ability to switch among styles has served me well, since every project offers up such different demands. In the last few years, I have been asked to design pool, lake, beach, and ski houses, country homes, city apartments, desert bungalows, and, of course, suburban houses, a process that brings me home full circle. ⑤

LEFT Young Scott's Magic Marker drawing of a Colonial-style house with double doors and a rooftop railing was inspired by a family vacation to Greenfield Village, a collection of historic houses at the Henry Ford Museum, in Detroit.

MY YEARS AT RALPH LAUREN

In 1998, I became the first in-house designer at the Ralph Lauren Madison Avenue store in Manhattan. My first full-blown project was for a lawyer. The client had fallen in love with a hand-stitched turquoise leather ottoman that had been displayed in the store's street-front window. He walked right in and hired us to decorate his office in a Southwestern theme. The crazy thing was, his Manhattan office was in one of the former Italian-palazzo-style Villard Houses, a series of brownstones designed in the late 1880s by the prestigious architectural firm of McKim, Mead & White.

The room, once the library of a townhouse, featured original wood paneling and other nineteenth-century details. I outfitted the interior in rustic browns threaded through with touches of turquoise. For authenticity, accessories like vintage serapes and antler sconces were purchased straight from the source—three fabulous shops in Dallas. The furniture came from Ralph Lauren: a gorgeous hand-tooled leather bureau, a glass-topped desk with sawhorse legs, and leather seating detailed with hand-stitching like a cowboy boot. The result was Northeast meets Southwest—I call it Cosmopolitan Cowboy. ⑤

ABOVE LEFT The aged-leather sofas and armchairs offer a rustic foil for the room's nineteenth-century carved-wood paneling. Neutral hues are accented with colorful accessories like the vintage serapes.

ABOVE The sofa's curved edges are trimmed with brass nailheads. Abstract-patterned Navajo area rugs are layered over sea-grass carpets.

OPPOSITE A pair of vintage turquoise pottery jars sits atop a Ralph Lauren hand-tooled leather chest.

BEACH HOUSE BAL HARBOUR

One day while I was working at Ralph Lauren, a woman walked into my office, which was in a beach-themed room called Summer Cottage. She had heard about my work and wanted to talk to me. She asked me personal questions, like where I grew up. I had no idea where this was going. Finally, she said that she had bought a 1950s hotel in Miami Beach, Florida, and wanted to do something a little different. "Maybe you and I will become friends," she said. I thought I would never hear from her after that. But the next day she dropped off a photograph of an Art Deco hotel in Florida with a note saying she wanted to meet again, this time with her family. It was signed "Mera Rubell" (I recognized the
name of the famous art collector and hotelier). At the appointed hour, she walked in with her husband, Don, and their children, Jason and Jennifer. They all talked at the same time, but instead of being overwhelmed, I was enthralled. They asked me to present guest room and lounge concepts for their newest hotel. The only guidance was the name of the hotel: Beach House. Even though I had never designed a hotel, we were a good fit because they wanted something laid-back and residential. The guest rooms would be a no-brainer: all blue, of course. Jennifer came alone for my presentation and flipped over the concept, and I flew to Miami the next day. It was the beginning of my wonderful eleven-year relationship with the Rubells. s

ABOVE Scott's first commercial project, the Beach House Bal Harbour, opened in 1999. All 170 guest rooms and suites were outfitted with the same white wainscot, faux-sisal carpeting, raffia headboards, club chairs woven from water hyacinth reeds, and Ralph Lauren striped bed linens.

OPPOSITE Rows of palm trees were installed around the existing pool, newly surrounded by sand-colored cement pavers laid with their smoother backsides facing up. Chaises are cushioned in a blue-and-white-striped Sunbrella fabric.

MY FIRST SHOW HOUSE

For the 2003 Hampton Designer Showhouse—which was held in Southampton, New York—I was assigned the pool area. I almost died the first time I visited the house: The pool was surrounded by an appalling redbrick deck. I thought, "What am I going to do with this?" After getting over the shock, it occurred to me that I could both complement and downplay the brick with a fire-engine red color scheme. The concept was probably a subconscious homage to the red sunroom in my aunt Rose's Ohio home. I began by choosing high-end fabrics. Some companies had just started producing much nicer, more decorative outdoor lines, and I was eager to try them out. After calling in red samples from every manufacturer, I narrowed down the selection to Donghia and Ralph Lauren. The teak seating was upholstered in solid red or white cushions with contrasting piping and accented with graphic pillows. Vintage wrought-iron chairs were rust-proofed with a coat of red automotive paint. All accessories were red, too: the custom topiary planters, the Coke bottles on the table, a pair of giant inflatable lobsters, and—for opening night—a pool boy dressed in red and white. s

LEFT The Southampton, New York, pool environment was bedecked in fire-engine red. Furnishings included lattice-back teak chairs from McGuire upholstered in Sunbrella fabric from Donghia. Floating in the pool are a pair of inflatable plastic lobsters (a nod to artist Jeff Koons' oversize crustaceans) nicknamed Larry and Lorenzo.

OPPOSITE The cushions were trimmed with a contrasting welt for a crisp look. The designer replaced the tent's existing fabric with a punchy red-and-white awning stripe to create an intimate poolside cabana for dining and lounging. The white-painted latticework transformed the pool area into an outdoor room.

TV GUIDE

JUNE 25, 2005

SPECIAL REPORT

SCOTT SANDERS

BRINGS FRESH AMERICAN STYLE TO TELEVISION

How You Should Be Watching T.V. Now

THE ULTIMATE RUMPUS ROOM

When I was invited to participate in the 2005 Hampton Designer Showhouse, the rooms were assigned by lottery. We were supposed to list our top three picks, but there was only one space I wanted—a second-floor bedroom—so I didn't bother to write down my second or third choices. Which, of course, meant I got the very worst room: the basement. I was horrified but determined to make it not *look like a basement. I painted the walls bright yellow, laid wall-to-wall sea-grass floor covering, and mounted curtains just below the ceiling to disguise the squat windows. My concept—the Great American TV Room—was a nod to my youth, which I had spent watching* Happy Days, The Partridge Family, *and* I Love Lucy. *The design was sparked by this great Sacco Carpet runner with yellow and avocado stripes—very seventies—which reminded me of* The Brady Bunch *house. We stitched together the runners, creating large area rugs to anchor the two seating arrangements. Online, I bought retro memorabilia like vintage lunch boxes and classic board games. The room was a complete sublimation of my childhood.* ⑤

LEFT Behind the Holly Hunt leather coffee tables are lamps from Crate & Barrel and chairs lacquered in green Maaco automotive paint.

ABOVE Near the television, Scott hung vintage *TV Guide* covers and one of himself made by artist Sean Mellyn.

MY GROOVY RENTAL

My 2004 summer rental in Wainscott, New York, was an exercise in redecorating on a tight deadline with a limited budget. The project actually started as a newspaper article. Jennifer Rubell and I were sitting around, dreaming up fun stories we could pitch to a friend of hers who worked at The New York Times *House & Home section. We hatched an article on interior design that was affordable and also temporary and minimally invasive, so you could remove it all when the lease was up and not tick off your landlord. The* Times *loved the idea but said I had to find the house immediately and furnish it within one week for less than $2,500. A real estate agent found me a fixer-upper: a run-down 1970s bungalow clad in dark wood paneling. I banished most of the furniture to the basement, repainted the bedroom walls, and raided Crate & Barrel and Ikea for art, accessories, and furnishings. The colors that season were bright oranges and greens, which were ideal for the retro scheme I envisioned. I styled the place in one day. My pièce de résistance was an installation of 1970s and '80s album covers that had been hiding in my hall closet since I was in high school: LPs by Billy Idol, the Police, INXS, Bananarama.* S

OPPOSITE The designer was photographed in the living room of the bungalow for a *New York Times* House & Home article on budget-conscious decorating tips for summer renters.

RIGHT Scott devised a clever means to cover a swath of the living room's wood paneling without damaging it: a colorful grid of vintage album covers from his high school and college days. The record covers were propped up on shelves made from inexpensive window trim, adhered to the wall via thin nails tapped into the deep grooves of the paneling so that the holes would be imperceptible when the installation was dismantled.

MY EARLY BLUE PERIOD

While studying interior design at Parsons, I moved in to a small one-bedroom in Manhattan's West Village, where I would live for thirteen years. The apartment was very Ralph Lauren, with a red-and-khaki color scheme and an unpretentious mix of antiques. It went through a few tweaks over the years. During my Burberry phase, for instance, I added plaid window shades and throw pillows. At one point, after ten years of the same look, I decided to redecorate entirely in blue. The particular shade I used was inspired by a box of Smythson of Bond Street stationery. I saw it and thought, "I want a room just like that!" The overhaul took about four weeks. As the grandson of a serial redecorator, I had learned the value of refurbishing pieces rather than replacing them. So I rearranged and reupholstered all the furniture, covering the sofa in Ralph Lauren periwinkle Ultrasuede and the side chairs in black leather for contrast. The only new items were pieces of blue-and-white Chinese export porcelain, which spruced up the kitchen cabinets and living room bookshelves. The result was like Auntie Mame in her Picasso Blue Period. [S]

OPPOSITE In 2004, after a decade immersed in a Ralph Lauren–inspired red-and-khaki color scheme, Scott chose restful French blues for his West Village one-bedroom, down to the Ralph Lauren fabrics and bedding. The navy wool blanket is from Frette.

RIGHT The makeover was documented in the September 2004 Color Issue of *House Beautiful*. A box of English stationery inspired the choice of new wall paint, Pratt & Lambert's Paradise Lost.

Makeover

WRITER: JILL KIRCHNER SIMPSON   PHOTOGRAPHER: MARCO RICCA   PRODUCER: DORETTA SPERDUTO

Out of the Blue

A simple change of color created a whole new look for designer Scott Sanders

AFTER

SOMETIMES ONE small adjustment can lead to a transformation. New York designer Scott Sanders had been living in his one bedroom apartment in the West Village for ten years when he decided he wanted a change. Always color-directed in his work, he took inspiration for his new scheme from the French blue of his Smythson of Bond Street stationery. When he found its match in Pratt & Lambert's Paradise Lost, everything clicked. His collection of blue-and-white Chinese export porcelain came to the fore and expanded; he re-covered his sofa in rich Ralph Lauren periwinkle Ultrasuede, and recast his bed as a rhapsody in blue. To keep the blue and white from becoming too beachy, he re-covered his chairs in Ralph Lauren's black Motorcycle leather. Crisp stripes, touches of geometric pattern, and contemporary art kept the look modern. >

BEFORE

A BIT OF SPARKLE

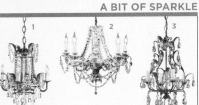

Chandeliers aren't just for the dining room: Sanders chose "the most masculine antique chandelier I could find" at ABC Carpet & Home to add a bit of sparkle to the living room. "Particularly at night, it gives the room a warm glow," he says. Other bright ideas:

1. Currey & Company's Laureate four-arm gold chandelier drips with crystals, $730.

2. This regal five-arm chandelier from Maura Daniel has an antique silver finish and crystal beaded swags, $750.

3. Vaughan's gold leaf and crystal chandelier has a curvaceous, airy leaf motif, $1,478.

R24		
1213	Paradise Lost Paradis Perdu	B1
1212	Colonel's Lady Dame du Sud	B1
1203	Daydream Rêverie	B1
1202⑥	Haze Blue Voile Bleu	DW
1245⑥	Cumulus Cumulus	DW

🅟 PRATT & LAMBERT

For continuity, Sanders chose blues that are just a rung away from each other on the color ladder: Pratt & Lambert's Paradise Lost for the living room and hall, and Daydream for the bedroom.

HB HINTS

GO WITH A FLOW In a small home, choosing a single colorway helps expand the sense of space and create flow from room to room. Sanders chose a slightly lighter blue for the bedroom, and a complementary stripe for the kitchen wallpaper.
LOOKING UP Painting the crown moldings (these were of uneven, poor quality) the same blue as the walls has the visual effect of raising the ceiling height. Using a cooler shade—blue, rather than the warm red, also made the room feel larger.
COOLING DOWN To offset the intensity of a strong color, choose a light rug, like the flokati in the living room (and the seagrass in the bedroom), and add lots of white in trim and elements like picture mats.

JENNIFER'S POOL HOUSE

After I completed the Beach House Bal Harbour hotel in Florida for the Rubells, Jennifer hired me to renovate her Miami Beach bungalow. She bought the house from the person who had built it in 1952, and the period details were intact, including the original turquoise Cuban floor tiles and a glass-walled living room that opened onto the pool. We took the fifties pool-house theme and just ran with it. The decorating process began at Toys "R" Us, where we filled two shopping carts with classic board games and inflatable toys. All the furniture was purchased from vintage shops in the Miami–Fort Lauderdale area and reupholstered or lacquered in high-gloss beach ball colors like red and yellow. The turquoise floors formed a neutral backdrop for the bold color scheme. Initially, tile was used only in the living areas, but we wanted to run it through the entire house. One of the only local companies that still made encaustic pavers, Cuban Tropical Tile, had discontinued the color in 1975. But a pigment manufacturer in Atlanta duplicated one hundred pounds of turquoise powder for us—enough to make three thousand square feet of tile. S

ABOVE The guest room's custom headboard and vintage bedside table were lacquered with yellow paint inspired by the stripe of a plastic beach ball. Short draperies and a piping-trimmed fitted bedspread bestow mid-century style.

OPPOSITE Full-height sliding glass doors and a deep roof overhang give the illusion that the living room is open to the pool. White brick walls are a backdrop for vintage pieces like the Knoll coffee table, whose glass top was swapped for a more 1950s-like Formica.

MY COZY COTTAGE

Two years after overhauling the bungalow in Wainscott, New York, I decided to rent—and redecorate— another summerhouse in the Hamptons. This time I searched for a home that had good bones and needed just a light makeover. I looked at three or four places in nearby Bridgehampton with Kate Tyree, a local real estate agent, but I wasn't into any of them. Kate's only other listing was a small cottage on a private lane. Because she had not yet seen the inside, she didn't want to show it to me in case it was a dive. But I convinced her to do it. We drove up, and it was the perfect little house—positively adorable! We peeked inside and saw this airy, whitewashed space with blue-painted floors—very crisp and clean. I totally flipped out and wanted to sign the contract then and there. I challenged myself to transform the tiny space by using only fabrics and accessories. Blue-and-green cotton-linen prints from SeaCloth gave the space a fresh spin. I bought a few woven stools and yellow side tables and then repainted my French wrought-iron chairs in bright blue. Cobalt blue glassware, which I find so summery and beachy, was the finishing touch; my collection follows me everywhere I go. ⓢ

OPPOSITE A painted ladder, propped near the front door, is used to display a collection of vintage tin pails from Amy Perlin Antiques in New York.

RIGHT The cottage was located on a private lane just off Main Street in Bridgehampton, New York. Black-eyed Susans line a gravel pathway leading to a front yard furnished with weathered Adirondack chairs.

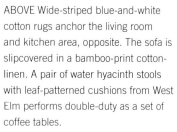

ABOVE Wide-striped blue-and-white cotton rugs anchor the living room and kitchen area, opposite. The sofa is slipcovered in a bamboo-print cotton-linen. A pair of water hyacinth stools with leaf-patterned cushions from West Elm performs double-duty as a set of coffee tables.

ABOVE A nautical-print SeaCloth cotton-linen bed skirt and a yellow lacquered Ikea side table perk up the small bedroom. The wrought-iron chair was repainted in blue automotive paint. Sean Mellyn did the gouache on paper, titled *Seaside,* in 2005.

OPPOSITE A collection of cobalt blue glasses and Saratoga springwater bottles brightens the open kitchen, which is furnished with a Ralph Lauren pedestal table, one of the few large pieces that Scott brought in. The watercolor of a pot was painted by Nancy Shaver in 1998.

HAMPTONS CLASSIC

Although this house in Bridgehampton, New York, was surrounded by farmland, the property lies quite close to the ocean and captures an amazing, pure light. But when I first walked through the rooms, the walls were painted all white and the house was completely bereft of detailing. The couple, who have three children, challenged me to create a sense of history where one did not exist: They wanted the year-old house to look as though the family had lived there forever. The goal was to bring down the house's newness and give it integrity without making it feel too grand. Their vision was something that felt cozy and unpretentious—a real home. A summerhouse should feel like summer, which to me means "beachy"! To make the water's presence felt, I dreamed up an entirely blue decor, deploying a number of shades throughout. I use blue in every project, but always a different hue—I've never repeated a blue! The pace was lickety-split—we had four months to fill fourteen thousand square feet. We purchased all the accessories, including three carloads of shells, in two weekend-long shopping sprees in the Hamptons. I love to accessorize a house and then let the clients buy what they like after they've had the opportunity to see everything in the context of their decor—and their lives. ⓢ

ABOVE The reproduction Chippendale claw-footed side chairs surround the clients' nineteenth-century dining table. A grid of framed botanical prints and a pair of Rose Tarlow Melrose House armchairs upholstered in periwinkle blooms pick up the wallpaper's floral pattern.

RIGHT To keep rooms from looking too matchy-matchy, Scott likes to offset pairs of seating by including a one-of-a-kind special chair—here, a leather-upholstered reading chair with a high wraparound back and nailhead trim from John Rosselli.

ABOVE Outfitted in sprightly red and khaki hues, the family room departs from the all-blue palette. The room's large size and square proportions posed a decorating challenge, which Scott solved with back-to-back Ralph Lauren sofas (one facing the stone fireplace, the other facing the television), an idea sparked by his memories of the living room in *I Love Lucy.* The hanging light fixtures are from Restoration Hardware.

LEFT To make the interiors feel more summery, the barnlike, double-height living room is awash in watery hues, from striped silk drapes to the azure tone-on-tone floral print of the sofa. Wool rugs from Sacco Carpet set off two seating areas furnished with dark walnut tables.

OVERLEAF The entry's hand-painted deacon's bench, a Pennsylvania Dutch antique from Nellie's of Amagansett, in New York, reminded Scott of one that sat on his family's front porch in Ohio when he was growing up. Flanking the bench are vintage cheese makers' crocks that have been recycled as a planter and an umbrella stand. Both are from English Country Antiques in Bridgehampton, New York.

A GLOBE-TROTTER'S LIBRARY

Invited to participate in the 2006 Designer Showhouse of New Jersey in Saddle River, I chose a room called the library, even though, ironically, it didn't have any bookcases! Luckily, I found a wonderful pair at John Rosselli. The pieces had very unusual lines: The ebonized woodwork was quite light, even delicate, which felt unexpected in a room where you generally find big, chunky pieces. I now had bookcases, but I still needed a theme. One of my assistants mentioned that she had one hundred and fifty vintage globes in storage, which sparked the idea to do a world traveler's library. We placed her globes everywhere: under the consoles, on the coffee table, and among the travel guides on the bookshelves. To curate a selection of paintings and photographs with a travelogue feel, I enlisted the help of Ruth Kaufmann, a distinguished grande dame with two doctorates in art history. Zebra-skin upholstery and African accessories lent the space an eclectic look. My favorite pieces were a pair of quirky English hall chairs with unbelievably tiny proportions. Hall chairs are really more about decoration than comfort—they are like sculpture. I don't think anyone was ever meant to sit on them! Only for show houses will I break my comfort-first rule. ⑤

ABOVE LEFT Ruth Kaufmann curated the collection of paintings and photographs featuring Zwelethu Mthethwa's 2003 *Untitled (Sugar Cane)*. A pair of zebra-skin-upholstered Ralph Lauren ottomans reiterates the safari feel.

ABOVE A wool-tweed area rug placed atop wall-to-wall sea grass creates a subtly layered effect and complements the mix of dark woods that includes a pair of ebonized bookcases and an antique mahogany chair with sinuous lines.

OPPOSITE With its turned-wood legs and scalloped apron front, this John Rosselli console is one of Scott's signature elements. The lower shelf offers ample display space for accessories—here, antique globes. The painting above the console is Jean-Léon Gérôme's *Return from the Lion Hunt* (1889).

OVERLEAF To emphasize the room's curved wall, Scott chose a round table from Amy Perlin. "A center pedestal is much more inviting than a table with legs," he says. Windowpane-plaid silk curtains play off the geometry of the mullions. The painting of a woman is an untitled 1940 work by Francis Picabia.

TOWN AND COUNTRY

Allison and Jeff McKibben, a young New York couple, wanted to create a version of a country house in the city for their growing family. They had bought two adjacent flats in a former Gramercy Park light-manufacturing building that had been converted into contemporary loft-style apartments. The catch was that the architecture could not have been less "country." The McKibbens gutted and combined the two spaces, added new moldings and wainscot to warm up the architecture, and requested furniture and finishes to make the high-ceilinged, open-plan space seem cozy. They gave me a blank slate: We were decorating entirely from scratch. They brought two leather chairs from their previous apartment, and that was it. I will incorporate a client's existing furniture into the new scheme when requested, but I like to go as far as they'll let me; reusing existing pieces can be challenging when you change aesthetics. Here we blended traditional and transitional pieces, all of which were kid-friendly—a Ralph Lauren sofa upholstered in Ultrasuede, a side chair done in a very sturdy cotton-linen, and leather used for everything else, from the ottoman to the dining room chairs. Upgrading to a larger space often entails building an art collection to fill up walls, as I did for a hallway off the kitchen at the McKibbens'. I'll shop for inexpensive pieces keyed to a certain theme—botanicals or shells—and arrange them in a grid or a salon style. For a smaller series, the mats and frames should match, but an all-over grouping frees you to embrace diversity. The mix of styles and mat colors offers an ad hoc effect, creating the sense that the pieces were collected over time. s

OPPOSITE Ralph Lauren tufted leather chairs pull up to a custom-made pedestal dining table. Scott assembled collections of vintage pottery—some pieces dating from the 1920s—for a number of rooms and grouped them according to color: blue for the living room, cream for the master bedroom, and jade green for the dining room. The pottery was purchased from Leo Design on Bleecker Street in New York, one of Scott's favorite sources for colorful retro accessories.

RIGHT The living room overlooks the dining area. White wainscot, colonial red wall paint, and windows dressed in striped silk Roman shades unify the two spaces. Blue accents, such as the pair of metal-shaded Wedgwood table lamps and the cashmere throw, add pops of color.

BELOW RIGHT The attention to furniture is evident in the living room's mix of wood finishes and chair and table-leg styles.

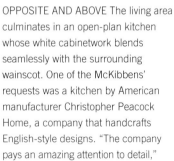

OPPOSITE AND ABOVE The living area culminates in an open-plan kitchen whose white cabinetwork blends seamlessly with the surrounding wainscot. One of the McKibbens' requests was a kitchen by American manufacturer Christopher Peacock Home, a company that handcrafts English-style designs. "The company pays an amazing attention to detail," Scott says, "yet the result is so clean-lined that it doesn't detract from the whole—or compete with the surrounding decor." White ceramic subway tiles are laid in a running-bond pattern. A trio of glass doors breaks up the monotony of solid wood fronts, adding a sense of depth to the cabinetry and offering display space for the clients' china.

ABOVE To liven up the long hallway between the kitchen and the bedrooms, Scott installed a grouping of equestrian and architecture-themed vintage prints set in unmatched frames.

A TRADITIONAL HOME

A former colleague from Ralph Lauren and her husband purchased a house in the heart of New Jersey's horse country. It's truly a country home, with a fall-winter feel that cried out for somewhat formal appointments and rich colors. Hired midway through construction, I was able to work closely with the clients to pick the kitchen and bath finishes—all the stone and tile—as well as a number of architectural details like moldings and fireplace surrounds. It's a big house, so it needed a lot of furnishings. My client let me select items from her old house. I chose the kitchen and dining room seating and, of course, the wing chairs, which I had reupholstered in a plaid wool from Ralph Lauren and then placed in the family room. The wall along the main staircase was a perfect canvas for a huge art installation. My client's only request was "No birds!" So I bought her a selection of drawings, charcoals, and prints of horses, gardens, and buildings. The installation process was, as always, quite spontaneous: My friend Sean Mellyn and I hung the art. He hopped up on scaffolding, and I handed him the pieces one by one, starting at the middle of the arrangement and working outward. We usually like to play off the color of each item, but otherwise we just follow our intuition. There are ninety-five pieces here, none of them particularly pricey or precious, and some that I paid only a few dollars for. The richness comes from abundance and repetition. ⓢ

LEFT Collections of cobalt blue glass, Chinese export china, and blue Wedgwood—assembled by the designer for the client—fill the dining room's built-in cabinet and echo the surrounding color palette.

OPPOSITE A collection of drawings and paintings lines the main stairwell. Blue and gold frames and mats, all from Skyframe in New York, reflect the decor of the adjacent living and dining rooms and unify the pieces.

OPPOSITE The fabric covering the dining chairs features the same exuberant paisley that animates the wallpaper from Scalamandré. Chocolate brown sea grass brings a neutral touch underfoot. Ralph Lauren wing chairs were upholstered in a blue velvet to match the dining room's silk drapes. "Texture adds much-desired warmth to dining rooms and guest rooms, spaces that are used somewhat infrequently," Scott says.

RIGHT Paisley patterns, also from Scalamandré, distinguish the living room. Scott designed the room around the distinctive fabric that covers the wing chair and throw pillows. The pale blues are complemented by azure velvet pillows and camel Ultrasuede. The custom rug by Vermilion completes the room. The antique chinoiserie screen is from Yale R. Burge Antiques in New York.

BELOW RIGHT In the farmhouse-style kitchen, rush-back bar stools pull up to a freestanding island, which is topped in chocolate brown granite to contrast with the white Carrara marble used elsewhere in the room. The lights, from the Oriental Lamp Shade Company in New York, hang from pulleys.

LEFT The bamboo bed and side tables that enliven the guest room are from Williams-Sonoma Home. The leaf motif of the duvet fabric is repeated throughout, from the botanical artwork to the tone-on-tone damask sisal and the textured, hand-painted grass-cloth walls.

BELOW LEFT In the master suite, pale gold was paired with light green hues and accentuated with chocolate brown to create a spa-like mood. To make bedrooms feel special and somewhat separate from the rest of the house, the designer typically chooses a color palette different from those of the surrounding rooms.

OPPOSITE In the sitting area, crushed-velvet love seats from Ralph Lauren are joined by a wood bench whose cane detailing makes the vignette seem more casual. The patterned gold-and-green upholstery inspired the selection of wall paint and other fabrics. Scott used silk pleated shades from the Oriental Lamp Shade Company to customize the chandelier from Williams-Sonoma Home. The crystal candlesticks on the mantel are from Ruby Beets in Sag Harbor, New York.

LEFT The clients' original wing chairs were reupholstered in a wool plaid for the den. The double-tiered wrought-iron chandelier was one of Scott's favorite decorative elements when growing up. This one, by Paul Ferrante, is nearly identical to a photograph of one Scott discovered in a file of tear sheets while visiting his parents in Ohio. The coffee table, ottomans, and étagère are also by Ferrante.

OPPOSITE A cluster of amber medicine bottles lines a windowsill. Scott bought the collection during an antiques run in West Virginia, where he was celebrating his parents' fiftieth wedding anniversary.

RALPH LAUREN REVISITED

In 2008, eight years after I left the company, my former associates at Ralph Lauren connected me with the builder of a private golf community in Palm Beach, Florida. The client wanted the model house outfitted entirely à la Ralph Lauren, from the paint to the draperies and furniture. In general, my aesthetic is pretty masculine: no diminutive furniture, no pastels—only bright, bold color. In a strange way, the decor of the house's library reminds me of my grandmother Mimi's zany, 1970s living room, which featured saturated red hues and a mix of wood finishes. This room is Mimi's living room filtered through a Ralph Lauren vernacular. [S]

ABOVE AND RIGHT For the Palm Beach library, Scott envisioned a quintessential gentleman's room dressed in head-to-toe Ralph Lauren, including a chrome and mahogany desk paired with an ebonized carved-wood and black motorcycle-leather armchair, both from Ralph Lauren, the red grass-cloth wall covering, an oversize black leather sofa, and a striking zebra-skin rug. "I like using inexpensive multiples to create a single design statement," Scott says of the grid of toy soldiers displayed in box frames above the sofa.

70

Chapter Three
The Dream Job

One of my most amazing projects came to me in a funny—but fortuitous—way. In May 2005, *Hamptons Cottages & Gardens* featured one of my interiors projects: a summerhouse in Bridgehampton, New York, that I had decorated in all different shades of blue. Samantha and Dan Anderson came across the article and flipped for the design. They were building a new home in New Jersey and wanted to hire an interior designer. Even though it was a weekend, they immediately called my office and left an animated message. They came in to see me a week later.

From the moment we met, I noticed they were incredibly warm and friendly. And totally all-American: They were very relaxed and dressed in shorts, like they would be popping out to play tennis immediately after our meeting! They brought along their architect's blueprints and a copy of the magazine article open to the living room spread. "We want you to do this for our entire house," they said. For me, it was a dream come true. The Andersons have an incredible aesthetic sensibility, and their style is very similar to mine—steeped in tradition but still lighthearted and youthful. They have two young daughters, Julia and Alexandra, and really wanted the house to feel like a true family home. It was one of those amazing projects in which the synergy was spot-on from the very beginning. Their enthusiasm for the project never let up over the course of four years. ⑤

LEFT A drawing depicts the Anderson house's front facade, clad in clapboard, stucco, and limestone. The Pennsylvania Dutch–style Colonial home was designed by New Jersey–based architect Cyril Beveridge.

THE ARCHITECT'S MODEL

During my first meeting with them, Dan and Samantha Anderson showed me the blueprints of their five-bedroom farmhouse. Cyril Beveridge's fantastic design sold me on the project. I was really blown away by the period details and authenticity. The design also spoke to my personal sensibility—notably, my love of Colonial architecture. Growing up, my mom always wanted to live in a Pennsylvania Dutch clapboard house. She had even commissioned plans at one point, though the house was never built. Working on this project was a little like coming home. The massing of the architecture is quite pleasing. I love how the house rambles around a bluestone terrace and encompasses a lot of square footage without even remotely resembling a McMansion. Cyril designed the house so that it would look like it grew organically over time—as though it had started as a barn and a main house, with a family wing added later to stitch the two original structures into a unified whole. That ad hoc quality is one of the things I've always loved about the genre, which Cyril captured so genuinely. S

RIGHT The architect's handcrafted model of the house shows that its exterior is designed to look like a cluster of smaller buildings, which breaks down the scale. "The Andersons specified that they didn't want a big house. All told, it's about nine thousand square feet, so I spent a lot of time making a large house look smaller. Much of that was achieved by careful attention to the scale and the proportions of the rooms themselves. The roofline is a unique aspect of this house. The roof is the same pitch on both sides but reaches down farther in the back, which makes the barn part of the house look like a one-story from the backyard. That way, you don't feel diminished when you're standing on the terrace," explains Beveridge.

THE ARCHITECTURAL PLAN

The floor plan is superb: the classic center hall, with a coatroom; the intimate formal living room; and the open-plan kitchen and family area, with their more meandering flow of spaces. The formal and family wings are connected by what's called a knuckle hallway, which bends at a slight angle. The beauty of the device is that it creates a sense of openness and connection between the two wings while providing some measure of visual separation. Because you cannot see all the way from one end of the house to the other, it feels more intimate. The interior spaces are also wonderfully proportioned. So often with houses that encompass a lot of square footage, the rooms themselves are oversize—which is one of my pet peeves. No matter how much furniture you put into rooms like that, you just can't make them look natural. The Anderson house is the complete opposite: perfectly scaled to human beings and the rhythms of everyday living. When we sat down to talk about interiors, the discussions were primarily about accommodating little "moments" geared to certain activities—things like a seating area for Samantha to hang out in while waiting for the laundry to dry, and a space for the girls to play or watch television in while she prepared dinner. I drew the decorating and furniture plan in July 2005, and I don't think the design changed one bit during the intervening years before the Andersons moved in. ⑤

HOUSE SPECIFICATIONS
- Square footage: 9,112
- Floors: 4
- Rooms: 21
- Bathrooms: 10
- Bedrooms: 5
- Garage capacity: 3 cars

RIGHT Beveridge's architectural plan of the first floor shows how the house reads like a series of three connected structures: the barn housing the garage, far right; the formal living wing, far left; and the family wing, center, connected by the angled, or knuckle, hallway.

OVERLEAF *The house is sited atop a slight swell in the land. It's oriented sideways so that the garage—detailed to look like a barn—faces the street, with the rest of the structure extending straight back from there. That alone is pretty fantastic: Because of this configuration, you can't see the road from anywhere in the house except the Man Room, a big entertaining space above the garage. The front of the house surveys a thicket of woods, while the back overlooks rolling fields and a pond—very pastoral and serene. Inside, the house feels wonderfully isolated and intimate. The property, which is a little more than three acres, is beautifully landscaped. The house wraps around a bluestone terrace, which has a pool. A low stone wall traces the edge of the terrace. The effect is like a floating oasis hovering slightly above the back garden.* ⑤

OVERLEAF As seen from the main road, the garage faces out. Photographed under construction, the home's unique design takes shape.

ANDERSON

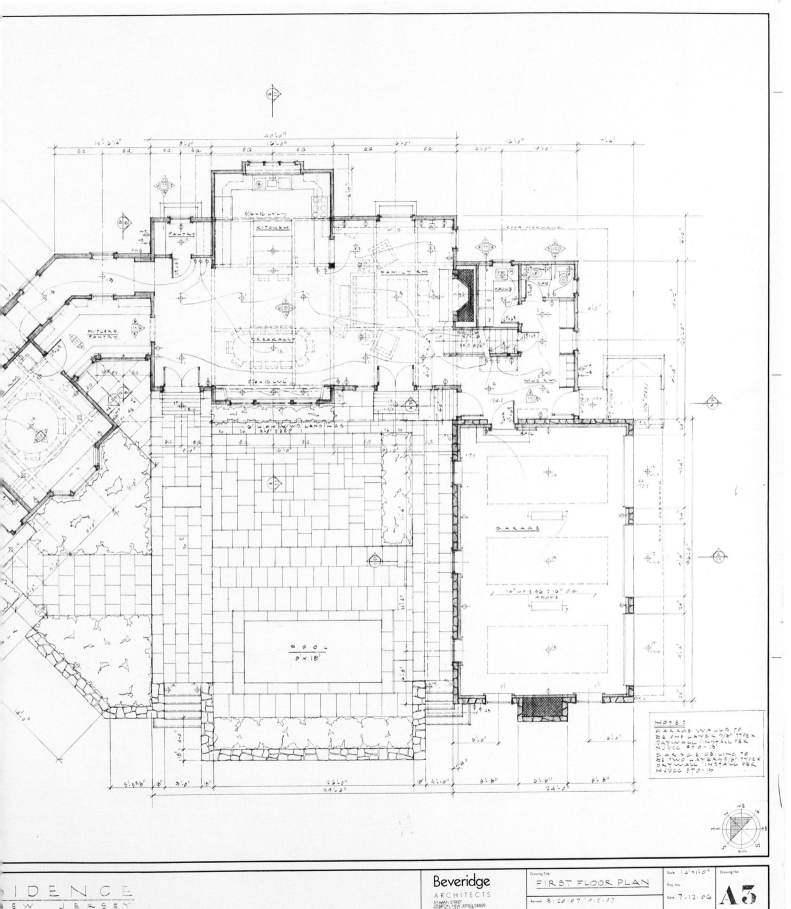

Beveridge
ARCHITECTS
55 MAIN STREET
CLINTON, NEW JERSEY 08809
(908) 730-8830

IDENCE
EW JERSEY

Drawing Title:
FIRST FLOOR PLAN

Proj. No.

Revised: 3·20·07 / 4·2·07

Scale: 1/4"=1'-0"

Date: 7·12·06

Drawing No.
A3

THE DESIGN PROCESS

Building and furnishing the more than nine-thousand-square-foot house was a four-year endeavor that included architect Cyril Beveridge's drawings and blueprints, the construction phase, and designer Scott Sanders' inspirations, floor plans, fabric selections, paint swatches, and furniture customizations.

Architect Cyril Beveridge stands near blueprints of the Anderson house, which line a wall of his former office.

Scott, Beveridge, and the Andersons discovered their mutual fondness for architect Russell Versaci's book *Creating a New Old House: Yesterday's Character for Today's Home,* a reference guide on period style that all of them had in their personal libraries.

The formal wing of the house, seen in this elevation, ends in a bluestone-clad library; the oval windows near the roof funnel light into the third-floor gym.

Scott's furniture plan of the living room shows the two seating areas and the placement of the consoles on either side of the doorway.

An elevation of the informal wing of the house shows the bay window off the breakfast room and open kitchen.

Construction began in March 2007 and took two years to complete.

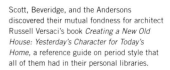

The team included, from left, builder Mike Scheier, Scott, and Beveridge, who posed on the back stairwell of the house.

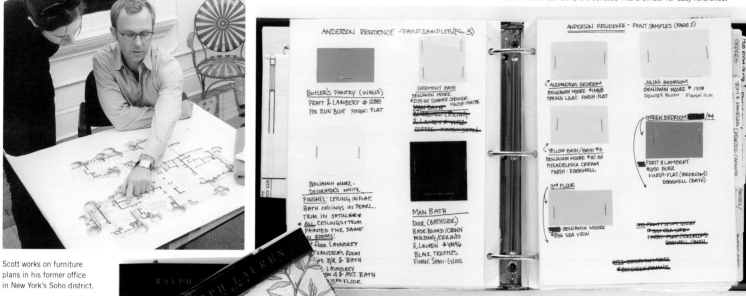

Paint samples for the interiors, including colors by Farrow & Ball and Pratt & Lambert, are collated into a binder for easy reference.

Scott works on furniture plans in his former office in New York's Soho district.

Dan Anderson gave Scott this tear sheet from a magazine to convey the cozy, clubby feeling he wanted for his private den.

Blue-and-white fabric samples from Ralph Lauren sparked the design of the Andersons' decor.

A glass bottle by artisan Elizabeth Lyons sits on Scott's desk in his Flatiron district office in New York. The framed floorplans, based on television sitcoms, are by Los Angeles artist Mark Bennett.

Scott's initial sketch, right, of the John Rosselli console in the entry hall includes a cluster of glass bottles on the lower shelf. (Later, Scott would place the pieces atop the console.)

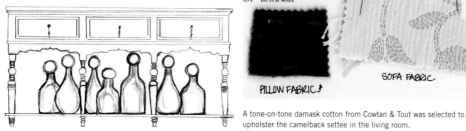

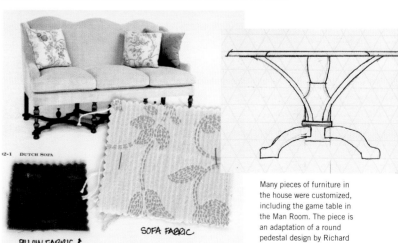

PILLOW FABRIC

SOFA FABRIC

A tone-on-tone damask cotton from Cowtan & Tout was selected to upholster the camelback settee in the living room.

Many pieces of furniture in the house were customized, including the game table in the Man Room. The piece is an adaptation of a round pedestal design by Richard Mulligan. Scott's assistant, Jennifer Rock, drew this rendering to show the desired octagonal top.

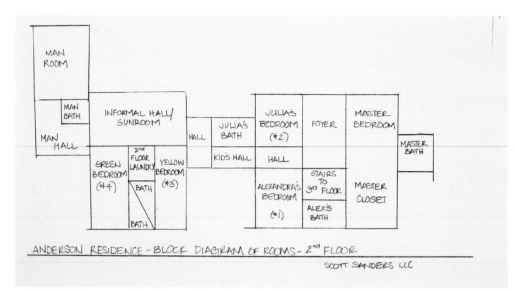

MAN ROOM

MAN BATH

MAN HALL

INFORMAL HALL/ SUNROOM

GREEN BEDROOM (#4)

2nd FLOOR LAUNDRY

YELLOW BEDROOM (#3)

BATH

BATH

HALL

JULIA'S BATH

KID'S HALL

JULIA'S BEDROOM (#2)

HALL

ALEXANDRA'S BEDROOM (#1)

FOYER

STAIRS TO 3rd FLOOR

ALEX'S BATH

MASTER BEDROOM

MASTER CLOSET

MASTER BATH

ANDERSON RESIDENCE - BLOCK DIAGRAM OF ROOMS - 2nd FLOOR

SCOTT SANDERS LLC

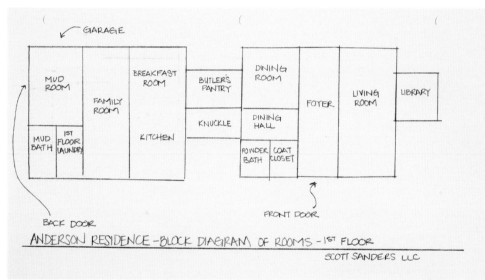

GARAGE

MUD ROOM

FAMILY ROOM

MUD BATH

1st FLOOR LAUNDRY

BREAKFAST ROOM

KITCHEN

BUTLER'S PANTRY

KNUCKLE

DINING ROOM

DINING HALL

POWDER BATH

COAT CLOSET

FOYER

LIVING ROOM

LIBRARY

BACK DOOR

FRONT DOOR

ANDERSON RESIDENCE - BLOCK DIAGRAM OF ROOMS - 1ST FLOOR

SCOTT SANDERS LLC

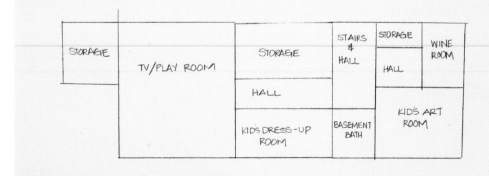

STORAGE

TV/PLAY ROOM

STORAGE

HALL

KIDS DRESS-UP ROOM

STAIRS & HALL

BASEMENT BATH

STORAGE

HALL

KID'S ART ROOM

WINE ROOM

ANDERSON RESIDENCE - BLOCK DIAGRAM OF ROOMS - BASEMENT

SCOTT SANDERS LLC

COLLECTING MATERIALS

The process of designing this house really honed my style. In a sense, it was the culmination of the residential projects I had worked on previously. Some of the houses I've decorated have been quite traditional, others have been very modern. But all featured my trademark strong colors and a common emphasis on casual, inviting spaces. And all mix traditional furnishings with contemporary art and fun fabrics so that nothing becomes too precious. The Andersons love classical elements, but because they are a young family they didn't want the house to feel stuffy. The project allowed me to use my signature elements and inspirations, though in an idiom closest to my own personal style—and thus close to my heart. Designing a house involves a lot of paperwork—blueprints, renderings, tear sheets, vendor forms, and even printed e-mails. To keep everything organized, my staff creates multiple binders for each project we are working on: one binder for decorating, one for construction documents, and one for communications with the client. The decorating binder is divided into subcategories for floor plans, pillow schedules, and delivery schedules. We're very orderly! We also have to file and organize swatches and samples, from fabrics and paint chips to tiles and faucet finishes. All those materials take up a lot of shelf space! One room of my office is devoted to a materials library, with industrial metal shelving housing storage bins for samples. The Anderson house is large: It had nine binders and five bins just for fabric samples. [s]

LEFT The Andersons' floor-by-floor block diagrams allowed Scott to coordinate his selection of fabrics, colors, and finishes by room and also by zone.

OPPOSITE TOP AND BOTTOM One space in the designer's office is devoted to storage for client files, including bins for material samples, all organized by room for easy reference. As a precaution, bins and files are kept for at least a year after completing the punch list—and even longer if the project is ongoing.

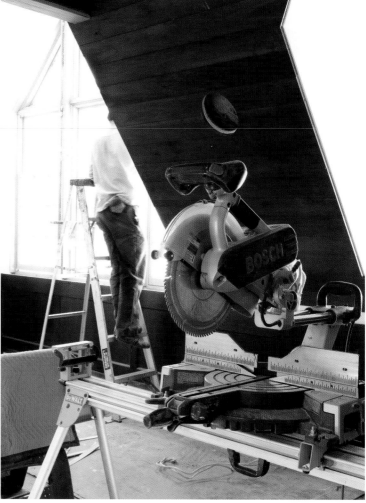

THE DECORATING BEGINS

Houses like this are such a team effort—so many subcontractors have to work their magic. The architect draws the plans, a builder brings them to life, and specialists like electricians and faux-finish painters execute the final touches. There's always one point in every project when all the elements are being worked on simultaneously but nothing is completed: Beams aren't stained, the wall and window trim is not yet installed, and the floors aren't finished. This is when I ask myself, "Can it get any worse?" I find it to be very chaotic—I almost can't even walk inside. But then it all starts clicking into place and coming together. We broke ground in March 2007. Once the process was under way, I visited every other week to attend the construction meetings. It was amazing to witness: The architecture had such integrity and warmth from the moment the structure was framed. The builder, Mike Scheier, is the best contractor I've ever worked with. He is a true craftsman, which is almost a lost art today.

ABOVE LEFT The large entertaining lounge above the garage, which Dan Anderson nicknamed the Man Room, is anchored at one end by a large bluestone hearth built by local masons. "Watching the Man Room go up was like being at a barn raising," Scott says.

ABOVE The walnut slats lining the Man Room ceiling were cut on-site.

OPPOSITE The room is distinguished by giant oak beams designed to mimic the look of a traditional Pennsylvania Dutch barn.

The entire top floor of the barn, above the garage, is occupied by the largest room in the house: a space for entertaining known as the Man Room. The architecture is arresting, with a ceiling that peaks at a rakish angle and culminates in a cupola with clerestory windows. Rough-hewn oak beams crisscross the space, and huge dormers flood the room with sunshine. I could have played off that sense of volume and light, but the room took a different turn. To temper the brightness, walnut woodwork clads the entire ceiling. The range of fabrics was chosen to reinforce a clubby atmosphere: classic patterns, such as tartans and checks from Ralph Lauren, in weaves like velvet and felt. The rich textures and dark hues combine to create a cozy refuge in the winter—and a shady retreat from the heat and sunlight of the summer months. ⓢ

ABOVE LEFT The window frames were treated to a dark-colored stain to match the surrounding woodwork. This window, in one of the room's four dormers, overlooks the bluestone terrace as well as the formal wing of the house.

LEFT The bright daylight is softened with dark woodwork that includes walnut slats lining the dormers and ceiling.

OPPOSITE The fabrics for the Man Room were chosen to create a masculine, club-like ambience: Ralph Lauren crocodile-stamped wallpaper lines an adjacent bathroom; Holland & Sherry corduroy covers a pair of wing chairs; and a classic Ralph Lauren plaid was chosen for the draperies, club chair cushions, sofa pillows, and a second pair of wing chairs. A custom rug from Sacco Carpets complements the room's fabrics.

CUSTOM WOODWORK

Samantha and Dan had a very clear idea of what they wanted for their kitchen: custom cabinetry from manufacturer Christopher Peacock Home, a company that handcrafts classical designs to mesh perfectly with traditional farmhouse-style architecture. The profiles of the moldings and the delicate articulation of the cabinet fronts look warm and provide the opposite of an antiseptic all-white kitchen. The same system was used for the butler's pantry, which opens onto the breakfast area and connects to the dining room. Between those two zones, the Andersons have tons of storage—which is any home-owner's fantasy! Whether planning built-in shelving or kitchen cabinetry, you should consider very carefully how it will be used—the items you need to store, as well as the exact amount of space they will take up. For instance, I always measure how many linear feet of books clients own to determine how much bookshelf space we need to build. We even measured the size of Julia and Alexandra's books to ensure we made their library shelves deep enough. The Andersons have so much cabinetry throughout the house that many of the drawers and shelves are still luxuriously empty—for now at least. No matter how much storage you have, you always fill it up! It pays to overestimate. s

ABOVE LEFT Elevation drawings of the custom cabinetry help guide the installation of the kitchen. The white-painted wood doors are matched by statuary marble countertops.

LEFT The window wall of the U-shaped kitchen has upper cabinets that extend almost invisibly behind the refrigerator and stove to create a lighter, less top-heavy look. Appliances other than the stove are hidden behind cabinet doors for a seamless appearance.

RIGHT The butler's pantry, which leads to the dining room, is built from the same cabinetry as the kitchen and includes a wine refrigerator and Sub-Zero refrigerator drawers.

BELOW RIGHT The girls' library features storage below the window seats. Rather than design lift-up tops—like those on toy chests—which would have required removable cushions to access, Scott maximized the space with drawers. They extend all the way to the floor, a neat trick accomplished by affixing the baseboard to the front of the unit.

HARD FINISHES

I adhere to a few rules when picking hard surfacing materials like floor tiles and countertops. Tile is permanent, so I generally choose colors and patterns that have a timeless quality. For a casual entryway, I prefer slate, since it feels warm and welcoming. I think it's important to choose neutral tones—white, even—for a kid's bathroom because children's tastes change so much over time. Don't be tempted to give your nine-year-old daughter a pink-tiled bathroom; she will just yell at you when she's sixteen! Bring in color via towels and accessories or with wall paint, which can easily be changed. In the master suite, bathroom finishes should be special and spa-like, to make it feel like a retreat. A subtly veined marble is a wonderful choice. In this house, the ground-floor powder room is covered in an exuberant chocolate-brown-and-blue paisley wallpaper accentuated by dark emperador marble. Because the half bath off the mudroom by the back door gets the most use, we installed bluestone floors. The basement bathroom is more of a hybrid: It's essentially another powder room, though that level's extra bedroom could be used for guests. So we included a full shower, lined in shimmery gray-blue ceramic subway tile. S

LEFT The downstairs bathroom has a walk-in shower with walls of tile from Waterworks in a running-bond pattern. The reflective surfaces bounce light around the windowless space. The floor is covered in a mosaic of earthy river rocks—great for a basement space.

OPPOSITE The tiles and stone used throughout the house include statuary marble slabs for the kitchen countertops, a basket-weave mosaic in the girls' bathrooms, and Walker Zanger recycled-glass tiles for the kitchen backsplash.

OVERLEAF Pages from Scott's binder include all the textiles for one bedroom on the left, while the wallpaper samples used throughout the house are on the right.

ALEXANDRA'S BEDROOM (#1 - PURPLE RM)

2ND FLOOR - BACK HALL

BEDROOM 4

BEDROOM 3

BEDROOM 2

MAN ROOM

SHAM - O+L - P # LF4391-03

SHOWER CURTAIN - C+T - P# J414F-04

DRAPES

C+T -
P# J483F-01

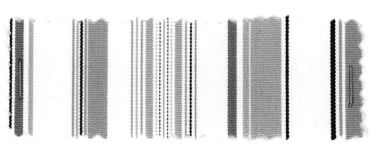

DUVET - C+T - P# J352F-02

Anderson Wallpaper Samples

Mud Bath
Elizabeth Dow
#3000-16 Prussian Blue
55"W
Sold by Yard

Coat Room/ Hall outside of Dining
Room/ "Knuckle"

Nina Campbell   #NCW2007-02
20½" x 11 yards /roll

Powder Bath   20½" rpt.
Osborne + Little #W5640/04   20½" X
                              11yds/roll

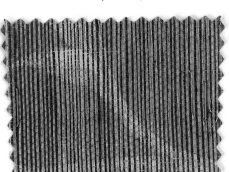

Dining Room
Brunschwig + Fils #U9480-200
34"W   34.25" repeat

1st Floor Laundry
Ralph Lauren #LCW30719W
Dune Stripe - Light Blue/Blue
27" W; Random Repeat

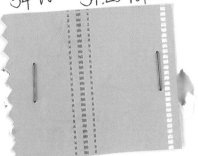

                           27"W
2nd Hall Laundry
Stark Wallcovering #5THT2193
Montgomery Stripe-Lime

                    36"W
                    13.5" V.R.
                    36.25"HR

Man Bath
Ralph Lauren LWP40879W
Yacare Crocodile - Mahogany

OSBORNE & LITTLE

OFFICE:
90 COMMERCE ROAD, STAMFORD, CT 06902
Tel: (203) 359-1500

SHOWROOMS:
SUITE 520, 979 THIRD AVENUE, NEW YORK, NY 10022
Tel: (212) 751-3333
SUITE 610, MERCHANDISE MART, CHICAGO, IL 60654
Tel: (312) 467-0913
SUITE 435, 300 D STREET S.W., WASHINGTON, D.C. 20024
Tel: (202) 554-8800
SUITE B643, 8687 MELROSE AVENUE, LOS ANGELES, CA 90069
Tel: (310) 659-7667
SUITE 435, 101 HENRY ADAMS STREET, SAN FRANCISCO, CA 94103
Tel: (415) 255-8987

SOFT FURNISHINGS

The Andersons have two daughters: Julia, who's seven, and Alexandra, who is three years younger. Their bedrooms were the last spaces I designed for this project. Even though I started thinking about them at the very beginning of the process, I wasn't quite sure which direction I wanted to take them in. So I set the rooms aside and cycled back a few months later. Samantha didn't want anything too youthful; she preferred rooms her daughters could grow up in. Although you can get away with a bit more whimsy in children's rooms, I generally stick with pretty sophisticated patterns. In the end, these spaces have the most transitional, classic fabrics in the entire house: butterflies and flowers from venerable textile houses like Osborne & Little and Cowtan & Tout. The prints are bright but not childish. When Julia and Alexandra are teenagers, the walls can be repainted in a neutral hue, which will allow the fabrics to take on a more refined look. Paint colors took some consideration, too. Julia wanted a pink bedroom. But again, I wanted to make sure the hue we chose wasn't too juvenile. So we picked a bright shade with a lightness to it, Benjamin Moore's 133 Powder Blush. It's not at all saturated—it's more like a wash than paint. When the sunshine hits the walls in the morning, the color looks four or five shades lighter. S

OPPOSITE This grouping of swatches shows the variety of fabrics chosen for Julia's bedroom, including an Osborne & Little animal print for the pillow sham and a butterfly motif for the duvet.

ABOVE RIGHT Julia's bedroom, flooded with morning light through two windows, stands empty prior to installation.

RIGHT Pale pink paint on the walls transforms Julia's room. Boldly striped carpets and drapery fabric from Cowtan & Tout ground the hue and keep the room young but not too frilly.

Construction took two years, wrapping up in the spring of 2009. It was a lengthy process, but that's what craftsmanship at this level of perfection demands. Finishing touches, like treating walnut floors with a dark stain and hanging light fixtures, are among the steps taken prior to laying carpets, installing window treatments, and arranging furniture. It's a treat to see the completed house empty, before everything else arrives. Then you can really marvel at the painstaking detail and the vision that go into realizing such a project. §

ABOVE The view from the living room through the central hallway and into the "knuckle" shows the empty spaces a few weeks prior to installation day. The wide-plank walnut floors have been sanded in anticipation of receiving a dark chocolate stain.

OPPOSITE The entry to the living room is off the front foyer. The crown and base molding in the central hall are painted the same color as the wainscot—Benjamin Moore's OC-17 White Dove in satin—while the walls are skimmed in a flat finish of Benjamin Moore's OC-40 Albescent.

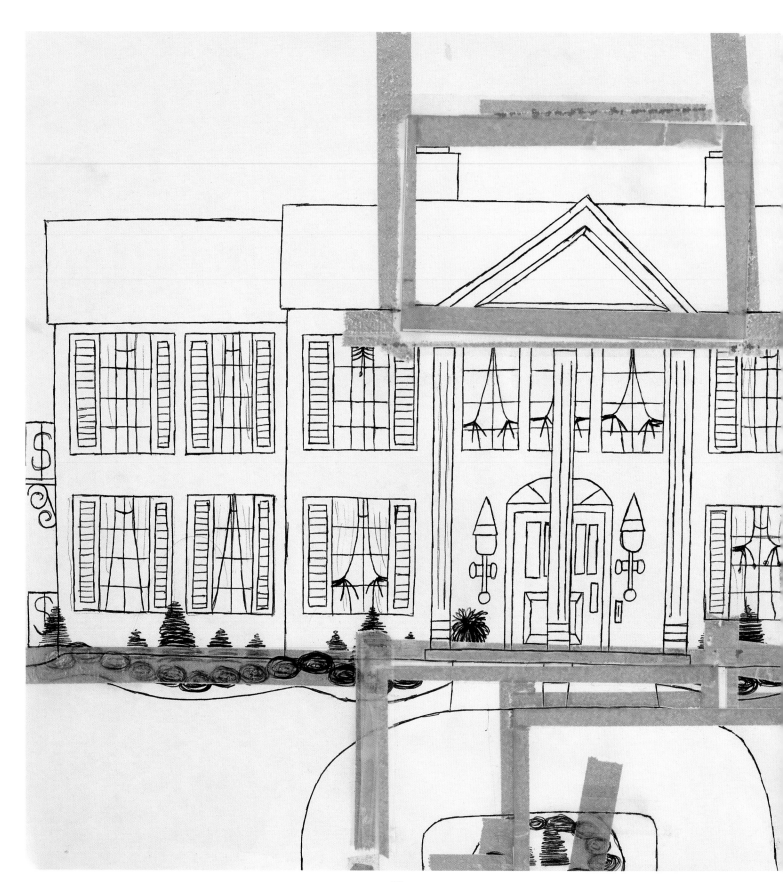

Chapter Four
Installation Week

Installation is always the most exciting part of the design process. It's important to be incredibly organized, because otherwise the move is a disaster. You *must* have amazing delivery people! And it also helps to start off the day with a *ginormous* iced coffee.

We had only five days to install the Anderson house—from the furniture throughout to the towels in the linen closet and the silverware in the butler's pantry—for twenty-plus rooms. The family left their old house on a Friday, flew to Anguilla for a vacation, and returned to their new home the following Saturday. It was a tight window, but I have my method down to a science. I've streamlined it into a five-day process in which I add a new layer every day: one day to move in the furniture, one to unwrap and start placing pieces, one to put together the rooms, one to arrange the accessories, and a final day for fluffing and flowers.

For houses still under construction, I ship everything to a single warehouse in advance so that all the contents are consolidated under one roof and arrive together from one moving company. I most often use S&S Warehousing and Delivery Service, which has a storage facility in Long Island, New York. If you have the means, this method offers numerous advantages: Because the warehouse receives, inspects, and inventories every piece, all items are accounted for and none fall through the cracks. After the clients have waited such a long time for their dream home, we wanted everything to be perfect the moment they step through the front door. ⑤

LEFT One of Scott's childhood drawings, a two-story Dutch Colonial, bears a coincidental resemblance to the Anderson house. In addition to tasseled curtains, he had also envisioned sconces shaped like an "s" (for "Scott") and a wrought-iron railing.

THE MAIN STAIRCASE

Many factors are involved in creating a lovely staircase. The treads should be wide enough to feel inviting, though narrow enough to convey a sense of intimacy. Natural light is always a plus; between the two doors downstairs and the landing window, this stairwell is blessed with ambient illumination. Typically, a formal main staircase needs to tell a formal story. If you have only one set of stairs, then it should be attractive as well as functional. The Andersons' front-hall stairwell was an interesting case because it's located in the heart of the formal wing but leads up to the family bedrooms. (Visitors take the back stairs to access the Man Room—Dan's dramatic lair—and guest rooms.) I generally advocate carpeting on stairs: It's less slippery, improves acoustics, and makes the treads last longer. Of course, you have to consider the amount and nature of foot traffic on the stairs before you install carpeting. Sturdy wool made sense here and allowed us to have fun with the design. Because the walls and paneling were painted white and cream, the carpet needed some color. Blue was the obvious choice, so we had a shade custom-dyed. Instead of trimming the runner with a tape border, I used the same plush wool as the carpeting but in a different color. The wonderful juxtaposition of the dark wood and the cream border really sets off the stairs. It brings you in and draws you up.

ABOVE LEFT The main staircase, which leads up to the family bedrooms, is located in the entrance hall. The front and back doors act as bookends for the space and flood it with daylight.

ABOVE Scott chose blue-and-cream-checked draperies for the landing. Since carpeting is installed before the furnishings are brought in, a tarp was placed atop the runner to protect it on moving day. The last element to be installed was the railing, whose dark stain matches the walnut floor and surrounding furnishings.

OPPOSITE The wool runner from Patterson, Flynn & Martin was custom-dyed a pale blue to match the draperies on the landing. Much deliberation went into designing the shape of the turned-wood newel post. "The profile had to be round, which I find so much more inviting and less aggressive than a square one," Scott says. "I also wanted the post and the handrail to read as a continuous line. We based this curvaceous form on a design that Dan Anderson found in a book."

THE SPREADSHEET

One of the secrets to a successful, organized move is to make a spread-sheet of all the items purchased for the house—an encyclopedia of everything, from side tables to sconces and throw pillows. Our list includes the vendor's name, the date each piece was ordered, the date it was shipped, and the room it's for. We give a copy to the warehouse so that their people can check off each piece as it arrives and label it according to the room it will be placed in. And we print out a copy for installation day, too; my staff and I stake out the front and back doors and check off every single piece that comes through. Then I cross-reference the lists to make sure nothing got lost en route. That task was especially daunting at the Andersons', whose list was seventeen pages long, with a total of seven hundred and ten entries! In addition to the spreadsheet, we always create a three-ring binder in which to compile all the information needed to furnish each room once the pieces arrive. The book includes floor plans, fabric swatches, and renderings of vignettes that show where accessories should go. It can become overwhelming to keep track of where every lamp shade belongs, especially in a nine-thousand-square-foot house that you designed two years ago! The design scheme included one hundred throw pillows alone. The spreadsheet and the binder combine to make a complete guide to putting together a house. ⑤

RIGHT The Excel spreadsheets list every item purchased for the interiors. Pieces are checked off twice: once when the warehouse manager inventories deliveries as they arrive, and again as they are brought into the house on the first day of installation.

Room#	ROOM	ITEM	MANUFACTURER/SHOWROOM	
1	Foyer	Accessories	Ruby Beets	Bottle stoppers
1	Foyer	Area rug	Patterson Flynn & Martin	5' x 8' area rug m
1	Foyer	Area Rug	John Rosselli/Vermilion	Tile Blue, custom
1	Foyer	Area Rug (runner next to stairs)	John Rosselli/Vermilion	Tile Blue, custom
1	Foyer	Area rug pads	Patterson Flynn & Martin	pads for Vermill
1	Foyer	Artwork	Pamela Williams Gallery	Dune and Cloud
1	Foyer	Artwork	Pamela Williams Gallery	Dune Dream 12
1	Foyer	Artwork	Pamela Williams Gallery	Heaven and Eart
1	Foyer	Artwork	Pamela Williams Gallery	Heavenly Dune
1	Foyer	Artwork	Pamela Williams Gallery	Sacred Dune 12
1	Foyer	Chandelier at front door	Remains Lighting	HL1483.18 Wins
1	Foyer	Console	John Rosselli/Paul Ferrante	2034- Charles Fr
1	Foyer	Console Table Lamp	Steven Sclaroff	# LT0495 - Pair
1	Foyer	Console Table Lamp Shade	Oriental Lamp Shade	Blue Mood Silk
1	Foyer	Settee	John Rosselli/David Iatesta	#23-0125 Regen
1	Foyer	Settee Pillow fabric	Kravet	#27656-516 Alig
1	Foyer	Settee Pillow trim	Samuel & Sons	#981-10665 Fre
1	Foyer	Side Chair	Holly Hunt/Formations	F-CH12S Canter
1	Foyer	Side Chair Fabric	Ralph Lauren	#LFY 23219F M
1	Foyer	Stairs to basement runner	Patterson Flynn & Martin	installed runner
1	Foyer	Settee Pillow fabrication	Martin Albert	4 16" square pillo
1	Foyer/upstairs	Sconces at landing	Carlos de la Puente	Single Arm Scon
1	Foyer/upstairs formal hall	Main Stairs and Landing Runners	Patterson Flynn & Martin	Custom wool rur
1	Foyer/upstairs landing	Drapery Fabric	Kravet	#24858-15 Miral
1	Foyer/upstairs landing	Drapery fabrication	Martin Albert	Drapery on Nick
1	Foyer/upstairs Lantern	Lighting	Vaughan	#CL96/M/N W
2	Living Room	Accessories	Sally Goodman/Jules Smith	One Large Blue
2	Living Room	Area Rugs	Sacco Carpet	Plain Field Colle
2	Living Room	Artwork	Pamela Williams Gallery	Sunset
2	Living Room	Bench	John Rosselli/Paul Ferrante	#6032 Scalloped
2	Living Room	Bench Fabric	Zoffany/Harlequin	#5462 Kira
2	Living Room	Candlesticks	Myrtle	pair of silver plat
2	Living Room	Chair (next to piano)	John Rosselli/Waldo's Designs	#6084 George II
2	Living Room	Chair (next to piano) Fabric Backing	John Rosselli/Waldo's Designs	backing of fabric
2	Living Room	Chair (next to piano) pillow	Martin Albert	16" x 10" throw
2	Living Room	Chair (next to piano) pillow fabric	Rogers & Goffigon	#92524-05 God
2	Living Room	Chandelier	Carlos de la Puente	6 arm chandelier
2	Living Room	Coffee Table (at piano)	Holly Hunt/Rose Tarlow	#2040 Inverness
2	Living Room	Coffee Table (between sofas)	John Rosselli	#0688 English S
2	Living Room	Console (2)	John Rosselli/David Iatesta	#13-0412 Sophia
2	Living Room	Console Mirror	John Rosselli/Michael S Smith	#810-1 Trumeau
2	Living Room	Console Table Lamps (2)	Oriental Lamp Shade	EB Silver, Candl
2	Living Room	Console Table Lamps shades (2)	Oriental Lamp Shade	08" Paper Empir
2	Living Room	Console Table Lamps- wiring charge	Oriental Lamp Z- mountings	Wiring of candle
2	Living Room	Drape Fabric	Kravet	#24858-15 Miral
2	Living Room	Drape fabrication	Martin Albert	Interlined Drape
2	Living Room	Drape fabrication	Martin Albert	Interlined Drape
2	Living Room	Fireplace screen	Wm. H. Jackson Company	6311HS - size: 3(
2	living room	Fireplace tools replating	A&R Asta ltd	replating of existi
2	Living Room	Ottoman (at piano)	TheShop(877.466:7467)/Gomez Assoc.	#51 Round Hall
2	Living Room	Ottoman (at piano) Fabric	Kravet/BarbaraBarry	#25386-5 Check
2	Living Room	Secretary	Carnegie Hill	English Small siz
2	Living Room	Secretary Chair	Huntting House Antiques	19th Century Re
2	Living Room	Secretary chair fabric	Ralph Lauren	#LFY 23219F M
2	Living Room	Secretary Chair-Reupholstery	Martin Albert	Reupholster hun
2	Living Room	Secretary Table Lamp	Oriental Lamp Shade	13 nickel candle s
2	living room	Secretary Table Lamp Shade	Oriental Lamp Shade	5 in Opaque pap

DESCRIPTION	QTY.	PAYMENT	ORDER #	Order Date	LEAD TIME	Received?
5 & 2 @ $575 (10% disc.)	1	100% CC	reciept# 251325	1/9/2009	paid in full 03/30/09	site
of foyer basement stairs runner	1	100% CC	dated 2/18/09	2/27/2009	in stock	
	1	50% Check	#DD18029	3/10/2008	SFA app 5/6/08 - arrival 8/12 - 8/26	
6"	1	50% Check	#DD18029	3/10/2008	SFA app 5/6/08 - arrival 8/12 - 8/26	
er, dining hall, and powder bath	1	100% CC	18268-GL	11/24/2008	in stock	PFM
	1	100% Check	#360	11/14/2008	in stock	site
	1	100% Check	#360	11/14/2008	in stock	site
	1	100% Check	#360	11/14/2008	in stock	site
	1	100% Check	#360	11/14/2008	in stock	site
	1	100% Check	#360	11/14/2008	in stock	site
	1	100% CC	#IN6424P	5/27/2008	Balance paid-holding shipment	S&S
Console, 72" W x 18"D, walnut CUSTOM	1	100%Check	#DD17891	3/10/2008	SFA app 5/9/08 - ship 8/29	S & S
amps w/ Nickle	1	100% CC	Invoice #1100596	11/7/2008	in stock	S & S
	1	100% CC	#501683	11/25/2008	in stock	S & S
P304 finish, faux ebony with rubbed accents	2	100%Check	#DD36586	3/10/2008	SFA app 5/9/08 - ship 8/29	S&S
	2.875	100% CC	#774028	8/21/2008	in Stock	MA
e #145 White/Blue/Blue	18	100% CC	#407478	8/21/2008	in Stock	MA
as per Baroda Console	1	100% Check 8/2	SO216812	3/10/2008	SFA approved 5/9/08-ECD 7/18	S&S
se- Cream	3	100% CC	Quote PL026	3/13/2008	in stock	Y
s	1	100% CC	dated 2/18/09	2/27/2009		
/2 yard each plus 2 yards trim each	3.6	CASH	#19379	11/14/2008		MA
	1	100% check	Est. Dated 5/9/08	5/27/2008	in stock	S&S
ue with cream border, nylon & coat closet area rug	1	100% CC	18290-GL	11/24/2008	custom	PFM
an	14	100% CC	#830776	10/7/2008	in Stock	MA
nterlined Nickel Hardware	0.9	CASH	#19379	11/14/2008		MA
antern, Medium, Polished Nickel	1	100% CC	#0049824	5/27/2008	20 weeks	site
are Pitcher	1	100% Check	#0149	12/22/2008	Pick up by Annie Hauls/ check #4103	S & S
34 8' x 13'6" and 11' x 16'	1	100% CC	#S2947KS-B	11/21/2008	TBD	Sacco
	1	100% Check	#360	11/14/2008	in stock	site
ize 24" x 15", medium walnut finish	2	100%Check	#DD36582	3/10/2008	SFA waived, ship 7/28/08	S & S
	5	100% CC	#0114565	3/17/2008	in stock	Y
ticks with copper showing through English c1860	1	100% CC	#10646	10/10/2008	in stock	SITE
dark chocolate brown walnut	1	100%Check	#DD17895	3/10/2008	SFA app 5/9/08 - ship 8/29	S & S
orge III chair	1	100%Check	n/a	9/5/2008	in stock	Y
	0.6	CASH	#19379	11/14/2008		MA
uppine	1	100% Check	#225594-00	8/20/2008	in stock	MA
	1	100% check	Est. Dated 5/9/08	5/27/2008	in stock	S&S
alnut w/2 drop leaves,2 gate legs, dark mahogany as #262, same	1	100% Check 8/2	SO216813	3/10/2008	SFA app 5/9/08 - ECD 8/25/08	S&S
48 x 31 x 21H	1	100% Check	#DD17885	12/12/2008	SFA app.7/29 / bal pd. w/ chk#2789	S & S
04 finish, faux ebony with rubbed accents	2	100%Check	#DD36587	3/10/2008	SFA app 5/9/08 - ship 8/29/08	S&S
nish: Antiqued Hand Rolled Mirrored Glass with Rosettes	2	100% Check	#DD22200	12/12/2008	in stock (check# 4080) bal. pd w/chk#2789	S&S
te- Pair Only	1	100% CC	#510610	11/18/2008	in stock	S & S
e - EB Silver, Candle Stick Silver Plate- Pair Only	2	100% CC	#510610	11/18/2008	in stock	S & S
to two lamps (EB-Silver, Candle Stick Silver Plate- Pair Only)	2	100% CC	#510610	11/18/2008	in stock	Y
an	58	100% CC	#717996	8/14/2008	in stock	MA
Polished nickel rods/rings/ball finials (Window # 3-5,7) 40 yar	3.6	CASH	INV# 19379	11/14/2008		MA
Polished nickel rods/rings/ball finials (Window # 6) 18 yards r	0.9	CASH	INV# 19379	11/14/2008		MA
park Arrestor with hidden screws in pol. Nickel	1	100% Check	4502	2/18/2009	paid with chk#4161/bal pd w/ ck#4144	
s in satin nickel	1	100% Check	dated 5-7-09	5/7/2009	check #4227	Site
ize 32"	1	100% CC	#5542	6/27/2008	6-8 weeks	S&S
	3	100% CC	#556923	3/31/2008	in stock	Y
t-top secretary	1	100% Check	dated 9/17/08	9/19/2008	in stock	S&S
r	1	100% CC	#1105	10/10/2008	In Stock	MA
se- Cream	1	100% CC	PLO39	8/19/2008	in stock	MA
1 - 1/2 yards	0.9	CASH	#19379	11/14/2008		MA
	1	100% CC	502578	1/22/2009	waiting for order to be ready	SITE
lor black white size 5 - for living rm secretary lamp	1	100% CC	502578	1/22/2009	waiting for order to be ready	SITE

Page 1 of 17

DAY ONE

This is the big day, when almost everything—furniture, accessories, lighting—arrives at once. The few exceptions here included pieces coming from the Andersons' former house, plus large furnishings for the family room and the Man Room. I typically start the day by giving the movers a quick tour of the house so that I don't have to run around with them every time they bring in something off the truck. I've been using S & S Warehousing and Delivery Service for more than seven years, and I know practically all the employees there by name! As an extra precaution, I also label each room by taping an eight-and-a-half-by-eleven-inch sign to the doorway. On moving-in day, the first step is to bring everything inside the house and put each piece in its proper room. It took six movers most of the day to unload the two trucks; we finished unloading by mid-afternoon—ahead of schedule. Once the trucks are emptied, the movers can unwrap pieces and return packing supplies—the mounds of cardboard, plastic, and blankets—to the trucks. Each unwrapped piece is then placed in its approximate location, to be positioned properly the following day. ⑤

OPPOSITE On the first day of installation, most of the furnishings arrive in two trucks from the warehouse.

ABOVE RIGHT The butler's pantry was mission control on installation day. Its location offered ample storage space for supplies, as well as a view into the family room, kitchen, dining room, and hallway.

CENTER RIGHT One corner of the family room became the lamp-staging area, where each lamp base was unpacked and then paired with its appropriate shade. Lightbulbs were installed later.

RIGHT The movers carefully maneuver a large item up the back stair.

SCOTT'S ESSENTIALS
FOR INSTALLATION DAY
• Cash for tips
• Lightbulbs
• Cleaning supplies including Windex, Guardsman furniture polish, soft cloths, and paper towels
• Paper booties for delivery people
• Trash bags
• Scissors and box cutters
• Double-stick tape for carpets
• Packing tape
• Black Magic Markers
• Snacks and water
• Camera
• Felt pads for furniture legs and accessories (so they won't scratch floors and tables)
• Tape measure
• Blue tape for cordoning off completed areas
• Step stool
• Picture hangers, hammer, and level
• Electric drill
• Lots of coffee and other types of caffeine
• A housekeeper to wash the new bed linens, make up the beds, and tidy up

OVERLEAF The majority of day one is devoted to unloading the trucks. Furnishings are carried in through both the front and back doors to save time. With a printout of the seventeen-page Excel spreadsheet in hand, Scott checks off each piece as it enters the house.

DAYS TWO AND THREE

On day two, three movers came back to finish unwrapping the remaining furniture and position all the pieces exactly where they belonged. It's very much a team effort: We go in like a whirlwind! If things go well on day two, then we can start placing the throw pillows on seating and the lamps on tables. We made great time, so by late afternoon the rooms had really taken shape. Day three is all about finalizing the placement of furniture and accessories. Amazingly, almost everything ended up working exactly where I had envisioned it would in the initial plans. A white Chippendale chair in the dining room needed a slightly different location. I originally wanted to use a set of the chairs as seating for the table, but the Andersons thought too much white lacquer would look overly slick. So we bought just one chair to use as an accent near the window. The day before installation, I said to my assistant, Jennifer Rock, "The only piece I'm stressed about is that chair!" I was worried that it didn't match the rest of the house. When it came off the truck and into the room, my heart sank. But when I moved it from the window to near the doorway, all of a sudden it looked fabulous—a note of eclecticism that brought the room together. S

ABOVE LEFT Painting is the first step of decorating, usually completed a week or two in advance of installation day so that the surfaces and trim have time to dry before wallpaper, carpets, and window treatments arrive. Nicks, of course, are inevitable. "You have to go back in and touch up the paint after the installation—that's just a fact of life," Scott says.

LEFT The dining room—with its walls papered and trim painted, window treatments installed, and area rug placed on the stained walnut floor—is ready for furniture. The white Chippendale-style armchair is from Baker. Both the drapery fabric and the wallpaper are from Brunschwig & Fils.

RIGHT The walnut floorboards in the family room were sanded before receiving a chocolate brown stain.

BELOW RIGHT To protect the newly stained floors during installation, layers of craft paper are placed on top. The cartoned lamps were grouped in the family room for unpacking and placing on day two, after all the other furniture was unloaded, unwrapped, and placed.

FABRIC CHOICES

Fabrics are my forte. Coordinating prints is a skill you either have or you don't—it's very hard to learn, though working at Ralph Lauren for so many years honed my ability to harmoniously mix and match different patterns and textiles. Sometimes I'll use just one fabric and repeat it throughout a small room. Other times, I'll carry a print from a sofa to a pillow, or a chair to a drapery. But I do like a variety of textiles in a room, as long as the space doesn't look too busy. Too many fabrics can appear dizzying and overwhelming! Limiting the palette to just two or three colors lends consistency. I also avoid contrasting color combinations. Instead, I like to pair pink with purple, or pale blue with spring green, as I did in the family room. After determining the palette, we shop different showrooms and collect a hundred options within the color scheme. We mix and match and sort and eliminate until we have a tight selection. Often, the whole palette is sparked by one fabric, and we find swatches to complement it. Occasionally, I'll go on a kick about a certain design, falling in love with an embroidery or toile de Jouy. A special statement fabric will give a room depth. ⑤*

OPPOSITE The textile patterns in a palette of blues and greens create variety in the breakfast area and the family room: The carpet is a striped wool from Patterson, Flynn & Martin; the stylized Kravet flower print was destined for a club chair; the traditional floral was made into kitchen valences; the Lee Jofa chevron stripe covers the window seats; and contrasting plaid tops the Rose Tarlow Melrose House chairs at the head of the Formations breakfast table.

ABOVE RIGHT At the end of day two, the family-room furnishings have been placed on the striped rug.

RIGHT Lighting was installed prior to the furniture, allowing large pieces like the breakfast-room table to be more easily centered below it.

THE LIVING ROOM

A number of steps require completion prior to furniture installation: painting walls; hanging wallpaper, window treatments, and lighting; and placing area rugs—all usually in that order. (Although, for the obvious reasons, wall-to-wall carpeting is installed before the drapes.) This sequence ensures that large furnishings are placed only once. After positioning a heavy sofa just so, you don't want to move it again to hang the drapes behind it! Plus, the electricians and window-treatment installers need wiggle room; installing drapery rods is a complicated task that completely shuts down a room. ⓢ

LEFT One end of the living room, where the piano and settee will soon be placed, stands empty prior to installation day.

BELOW LEFT By the end of day one, the secondary seating area of the living room has been filled with furniture. Window treatments and rugs were installed before the piano arrived to avoid moving heavy pieces twice.

The sliver of space between the two front windows in the living room presented a challenge. Normally I would have placed a console there, but I had already used two in the room. I had a vision of my grandmother writing at her antique secretary in her formal living room, so I became fixated on finding one just like it to fit this tall, skinny space. A contemporary design was out of the question, since they are usually overscale. So I scoured every antiques shop under the sun. Many months passed before I found this miniature English Chippendale secretary—it's rare to find one so petite. When we placed it on the front wall during moving day, it filled the space perfectly, as though it had been custom-designed. ⑤

RIGHT Painting the walls with Farrow & Ball Parma Gray No. 27, a silvery blue, gave the room a sense of dimension and made the white trim pop out.

BELOW RIGHT Before the furniture was in place, the elegant architecture of the living room, with its coffered ceiling and daylight streaming in through corner windows, took center stage. The light, airy feeling is preserved by daintily proportioned pieces: the secretary on the front wall; a wood armchair beside it; and the low benches, used in place of armchairs, by the fireplace.

SOFT OPTIONS

Mattresses arrive on the second day, after the bed frames have been assembled and put in place. Making the beds is quite an effort; all the bed linens and towels need to be washed and ironed. Every bedroom gets two sets of custom linens, including bed skirts and European shams. We had them made by Martin Albert Interiors, the company that oversaw the draperies, Roman shades, window-seat cushions, and upholstery. It makes sense to consolidate the soft goods: The house had about a hundred throw pillows and fourteen window-seat cushions, all with trim—a staggering amount of fabric! [S]

LEFT Younger daughter Alexandra's bedroom awaits a coat of purple paint prior to installation.

BELOW LEFT Once hung, the floral draperies brighten the bedroom. Mattresses and bedding arrive at the end of the second day, after bed frames are assembled in their proper places.

RIGHT The yellow guest room is filled with light—and little else—before the draperies and wall fabric were installed.

BELOW RIGHT In the guest room a week later, yellow toile fabric was upholstered onto the walls, matching draperies were hung, and the striped carpet was laid, all in anticipation of the arrival of the bed and nightstands.

CROWNING GLORY

Except for a few special pieces, the chandeliers, hanging lights, sconces, and other lighting fixtures are installed by the electrician in advance of installation day. Because the furniture for the Man Room was slated to arrive on a Tuesday, we had time to install the chandelier on Monday. Hoisting that piece thirty feet in the air proved a nearly all-day—and slightly dizzying—affair. Once up, the wrought-iron design looked amazing against the rough, walnut-stained oak beams and exposed-steel bolts. Picking the right fixture for that spot was tricky. Because the wood cladding gives the elegant, sophisticated room a certain rusticity, a very fine or shiny fixture would have stood out. The grandness of the multi-tiered chandelier, which looks like it was salvaged from an old castle, comes from its geometry and scale. Recently, I flipped through a file of pages I had torn from decorating magazines when I was little, and I found a country-inspired room with an almost exact replica of this fixture—another subconscious nod to my childhood. ⑤

RIGHT It took three people to raise the Paul Ferrante wrought-iron chandelier in the cupola of the Man Room.

OVERLEAF *On day four, we brought in the plants, mostly colorful orchids. Sometimes we would run out to buy a last-minute accessory to fill in a small hole. The styling process typically continues even after the house is inhabited, so that I can see how the clients use the space. But otherwise, moving week wraps on day five. We add the final touches and then block off each room with a strip of blue tape and a DO NOT ENTER sign. It's very cathartic to put the house to bed, close down the design, and pass it onto the clients.* ⑤

OVERLEAF From the silk rug to the orchids, the living room was the first space to be fully finished.

DO NOT ENTER

UNLESS YOU HAVE

CLEAN BOOTIES!

Chapter Five
The Finished House

One of my primary concerns for the Anderson home was that the interior design be authentic to the architecture. Cyril Beveridge, the architect, did such an incredible job of replicating the details of a Pennsylvania Dutch house that it was important to emphasize his intention with the decor. Yet I didn't want to be slavish to the Colonial vernacular; it was more about capturing a *feeling* of authenticity and old-world values than trolling through design-history books to re-create a period look. The furniture style appropriate to the house happens to be what I love best: an amalgam of influences, from Early American and nineteenth-century English to classic Ralph Lauren. The rooms combine antiques and reproductions, all graced with a subtle, elegant patina. I gravitated to solid-wood furniture with gorgeous graining but otherwise very little ornamentation. Accessories were purchased during a series of shopping trips and then layered into the design to look as though they had been collected over time. Fabrics feature timeless prints—stripes, plaids, damasks, and toiles—enlivened by a few whimsical touches. The house is big, so it needed a lot of color changes, but blue ties it all together. The design balances similarity and difference—the palette is cohesive throughout but shifts from room to room; elements such as lighting have a common sensibility even though the forms vary. That's my style: clean and organized yet energized with enough variety so that it doesn't feel homogenous. It may sound easy to pull off, but it's not. ⒮

LEFT A young Scott's imaginary home, executed in colored marker, features high-end essentials like private terraces, a pool surrounded by a deck with stream-lined furnishings, and his initial on the chimney.

MAKING AN ENTRANCE

The front hall is an in-between space. To the right is the all-blue living room. Straight ahead is the formal staircase. And to the left is a corridor, wallpapered in blue and cream stripes, leading to the dining room and the family wing. With so much color in those surrounding spaces, the entry needed to be a serene, calm presence to the eye. But it still has a quiet personality all its own. Morning light floods this part of the house, especially through the leaded-glass windows on either side of the front door. I ran with that bright, airy feeling by painting the walls cream and the wainscot white. Finding a good cream paint is exceedingly tricky. Too much of an undertone can make a cream turn green or pink, but too little color is really just an off-white, which lacks depth and is a little dull. It took a lot of trial and error and on-site testing to find a cream with the right richness and character. This one—Benjamin Moore's OC-40 Albescent—pairs beautifully with the dark wood furnishings, including my signature console, a turned-wood hall chair, and the ebonized benches flanking the door. The accessories—striped pillows and giant blue glass decanters—are teasers of the neighboring spaces, a preview, like the foyer itself, of what's to come.

ABOVE LEFT Topping the console in the front hall, custom-colored glass decanters reflect the light that floods in from every angle. The grouping was inspired by Scott's mother, who collects glass bottles. The pieces were made by sculptor Elizabeth Lyons and came from Ruby Beets, a shop in Sag Harbor, New York.

ABOVE Inside the front door, ebonized benches with woven-cane seats by David Iatesta strike the desired balance between formal and casual. Above each bench is a photograph of a pastoral African landscape, *Mulanje Malawi Tea Estate* (1999) by artist Jackie Nickerson, from the Jack Shainman Gallery in New York; the photographs read almost as windows, thus intensifying the room's indoor-outdoor quality.

OPPOSITE Floored in bluestone, the mudroom by the back door leads to the family wing. The angled base of the console from Formations plays off the vertical slats of the beadboard paneling on the walls and ceiling. Above is Joshua Marsh's 2008 oil-on-panel *Pitcher (Yellow)*, from the Jeff Bailey Gallery in New York. The antique umbrella stand is from Huntting House Antiques in East Hampton, New York.

THE FINISHED LIVING ROOM

It is generously sized but not huge, so furnishings were chosen with an eye for scale and proportion. Using benches instead of armchairs near the sofas kept the main seating vignette from feeling too crowded. Moreover, a chair would have turned its back to the room—quite uninviting. Usually, the location of doors guides the placement of furniture in a room. But here the doorway from the entry hall into the living room is not exactly on center, which creates a somewhat asymmetrical configuration. To instill a sense of balance and symmetry, I placed a pair of consoles on either side of the doorway, thus framing the view as you look back out into the hall. Porcelain jars on the lower shelves of the consoles bring the eye down. I love to arrange tableaux of objects with similar hues or sensibility; everything in life should be arranged by color! s

PREVIOUS PAGES In the living room, pairs of furnishings—damask-covered sofas from O'Henry House, consoles, and nailhead-trimmed scalloped benches by Paul Ferrante—are rounded out by solo statement pieces that include the wing chair in a corner and the antique secretary. The windows are draped in pinch-pleated Kravet silk drapes. The wing chair in the corner is upholstered in a Zoffany fabric.

LEFT Over each console by David Iatesta, a gold-leafed mirror draws attention upward, while a cluster of porcelain jars from English Country Antiques in Bridgehampton, New York, creates visual interest closer to the floor.

RIGHT A polished-nickel urn lamp mingles with an antique Wedgwood pitcher purchased during a shopping trip to Bucks County, Pennsylvania, in search of accessories suited to the home's Dutch Colonial architecture. Covering the throw pillow is a pale blue silk-viscose from Cowtan & Tout that matches the paint color of the walls. "I love the raised beige embroidery, which lends depth and texture," Scott says.

PROPER PAIRS

A cautionary tale: When buying two identical custom pieces, specify that they will be used as a matching pair. For instance, the antiqued, gold-leafed mirrors for the living room consoles arrived with quite different patinas. That would have been fine if they were going in separate parts of the house, but these would be making a specific point about symmetry! The fabricator wanted to take one back and faux-age it a little more, but it's almost impossible to get an identical set unless the pieces are made together. So we convinced them to craft us a new pair.

I wanted to use just two colors in the living room; the restrained palette is what the Andersons responded to in the photograph that inspired the design of this house. We chose blue paint for the walls, so for contrast we went with cream for the carpet and fabrics. I selected a silk carpet because it's a little dressy but still cozy. I didn't want the room to come off as too stiff. The subtle sheen plays nicely off the flat finish of the walls and the tone-on-tone damask covering the sofas. The upholstery has depth and texture but reads as a solid from a distance. Centering the main seating area on the hearth left a little extra space to fill at the back of the room. A camelback love seat near the piano carves out a more intimate vignette for listening to music. The room gets a lot of use, not only for parties but also for impromptu performances: The Andersons' older daughter, Julia, takes lessons and practices a few times a week. It's a living room to be lived in. ⓢ

ABOVE A camelback settee from John Rosselli defines the seating area in the rear corner of the living room. The button-tufted ottoman and the wheeled, English reading-room chair can be easily rearranged for parties or piano performances. The fabrics, embroidered cotton and cotton damask embellished with minimal trim, are elegant but not precious.

RIGHT Surrounding the fireplace, the main seating area features a pair of sofas covered in a Cowtan & Tout tone-on-tone wool-silk damask, all grounded by a silk rug from Sacco Carpet. Above the hearth is a trio of oil-on-linen canvases from Janet Jennings' 2008 *Dune* series, purchased from the Pamela Williams Gallery in Amagansett, New York.

THE FINISHED DINING ROOM

The Andersons requested a "sexy" dining room. No one has ever asked me to do such a thing before, so it took some thinking! "Sexy" could have been translated into dark colors, but that would have jarred with the rest of the decor, which is all about light hues and shades of blue. When I considered how the space would be used—mostly at night, lit dimly or by candlelight—shimmery fabrics and rich textures came to mind. A tone-on-tone silk rug, soft blue chenille seating, and grass-cloth walls make the space feel intimate yet informal, while metallic finishes—the gold-striped silk drapes, a mirrored silver-leafed cabinet, the antiqued-nickel lantern—imbue the space with low-key glamour. In a dining room, you need ample surface area for serving pieces. But when the room is not used, empty credenzas and tables can look desolate. The key is to have just a handful of big, sculptural pieces rather than a lot of small odds and ends. ⓢ

OPPOSITE Touches of gold abound, from the silk drapes to the handblown decanters by Elizabeth Lyons. The round table and the antiqued-nickel fixture came from Holly Hunt.

RIGHT Grass cloth from Brunschwig & Fils brings texture to the dining room walls. Atop the mirrored cabinet by John Rosselli are handblown pears by Ann Wright from Nellie's of Amagansett, New York.

OVERLEAF On the console from Rose Tarlow Melrose House, in Los Angeles, is Sean Mellyn's mixed-media-on-paper *Giverny Serving Tray* (2008), inspired by his fellowship at the Fondation Claude Monet in Giverny, France. The frame is by Handmade Frames. The Reichenbach porcelain updated by Paola Navone is from Jarlath Mellett in Amagansett. The Ralph Lauren nickel lamps have pleated silk shades from the Oriental Lamp Shade Company.

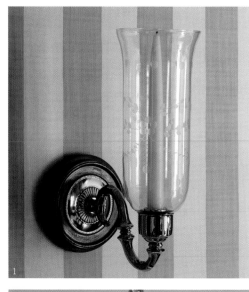

LIGHTING CHOICES

In a traditional-style home, you can't use high-hat and recessed lighting everywhere; you need real fixtures with presence and a sculptural sensibility. Luckily, the Andersons hate flush mounts as much as I do, and they love lanterns. We would have used them in every room, but that would have been a bit much. So I mixed in drop pendants, sconces, and chandeliers. Mixing antique and modern pieces keeps a house from looking like a lighting showroom. Remains Lighting in New York is one of my go-to resources for both old and new designs; we purchased a number of antiques there, including the 1920s quilted mercury glass pendants in the butler's pantry. Vaughan is another favorite supplier of upscale lighting with a historic flair. The challenge was to bring in enough variety to keep the spaces from looking repetitious and yet maintain a sense of cohesion through the house. We had a lot of variety in terms of form but stuck with similar finishes—nickel, silver, or oil-rubbed bronze. I also sourced many table-lamp bases: glass, turned wood, nickel, chrome, Art Deco, and antique urns. ⑤

OPPOSITE FROM TOP LEFT The variety of lighting includes (1) an Architrove candlestick sconce with cut-glass hurricane; (2) a Vaughan delicate mouth-blown glass globe wrapped in handwoven nickel wire; (3) a polished-nickel hurricane sconce, also by Vaughan; (4) a 1920s blue mercury glass pendant from Remains Lighting; (5) a 1930s copper mercury glass pendant, also from Remains Lighting; (6) a glass pendant from Wyeth; (7) a traditional polished-nickel lantern from Vaughan; (8) a Paul Ferrante globe; (9) and an octagonal bronze fixture.

RIGHT The antiqued-nickel lantern from Formations is unusual in the dining room, where a chandelier is a more expected choice.

THE HEART OF THE HOUSE

The kitchen is the center of a classic farmhouse. Here it is combined with the breakfast area and the family room to form the largest space in the house. The bigger the space, the more fabrics are required. An open plan like this, which is really three rooms in one, begs for careful coordination. In the breakfast area alone, we had two types of chair upholsteries, plus the Roman shades and window-seat cushions to consider. To make the rooms read as one unified zone, it was vital that the colors and the patterns coordinate, though a bit of differentiation was needed from the breakfast area to the family room proper. I like the palette to be tight—just two or three hues; I prefer eclecticism to come from the furniture rather than color. By sticking with just blue and green, we were able to mix checks, stripes, and plaids for variety. The family room features slightly bolder patterns, like a stylized floral from Kravet, while the breakfast-area prints are somewhat subtler. [S]

LEFT AND OPPOSITE A cluster of new and vintage glass bottles, some purchased in France, creates a dramatic moment on the breakfast-room table. "A collection of similar objects reads as a single gesture while offering the effect of a multiple," Scott says. Formations' distressed table is mixed with DeWinter sidechairs from Richard Mulligan in California.

OVERLEAF Fabrics in the same blue-and-green palette create continuity between the breakfast area and the family room, while furniture placement gives each space its own identity. "Open floor plans are challenging," Scott says. "It's important to divide the space into several intimate areas without making it seem too compartmentalized." Scott faced the chairs away from the breakfast area to carve out a more intimate seating group around the fireplace. The unusual coffee table with pull-out shelves is from Rose Tarlow Melrose House.

Because the family room is anchored by a huge stone fireplace, the decor required a degree of rusticity. But the space itself is quite small. In terms of furniture, it's basically just a chair, a sofa, and a coffee table. So any rough-hewn quality needed to come from other elements. Selecting the seating was easy: Years ago, I had fallen for Richard Mulligan's DeWinter chair, and I now knew that a set of them would make this whole space. The rush-seat detail tempers the formality, while the armrests feature a rubbed-off finish that offers just the right dose of patina. They are also the most comfortable chairs imaginable—everyone loves sitting in them! Lighting proved trickier. I debated what sort of piece would work best. I had already used a lot of lanterns throughout the house—including one above the breakfast table—so for variety, a chandelier made more sense. Fortunately, I found this amazing wrought-iron fixture with a wood stem to provide the perfect balance of informality and structure. The Andersons weren't sold on the chandelier when I showed it to them. I begged them to trust me on this one—I just knew it would fill up the room perfectly, and it did. s

OPPOSITE The ebonized chair is from Los Angeles designer Richard Mulligan, who crafts reproductions of Early American pieces.

ABOVE A Paul Ferrante wrought-iron and wood chandelier illuminates the family room. Its eight curved arms appear to hold real candles.

A CLASSIC KITCHEN

The kitchen—a Christopher Peacock Home design—is an all-white affair: white-painted cabinetry, a creamy recycled-glass-tile backsplash, and countertops of white statuary marble, which was chosen for its very subtle, almost imperceptible veining. To invite contrast, we topped the center island in lustrous teak. The finish is a chocolate brown with a hint of red to complement—but not quite match—the breakfast-room table. I also like the combination of marble and granite in a kitchen: Granite is the most user-friendly, lowest-maintenance surface for hard-core cooks, and it creates nice variety in an otherwise white-on-white decor. Accessorizing the kitchen is an often overlooked step. Even though it may be the most utilitarian room of the house, the kitchen still needs a decorative touch, since you inevitably spend so much time there. And an all-white space, especially, calls out for jolts of color. In the kitchen, as in the dining room, you want to focus on a few big objects that are both pretty and functional—and that can easily be stored when you need the counter space to prepare a large meal. I selected a green glass fruit bowl, glass jars filled with colorful candy, and topiaries in terra-cotta pots. There's one swath of countertop that, courtesy of its location, is visible from every part of that wing— the breakfast room, the hallway, the butler's pantry, and the family room. So it needed a statement piece, something special. Every time I visited Samantha, she would set out a plate of fresh-baked cupcakes or cookies, so I bought her an antique-looking cake stand from home, james!, a store in East Hampton, New York. Luckily, the shop had one in a gorgeous blue! ⓢ

OPPOSITE To bring contrast to an otherwise white-on-white scheme, the kitchen island is topped in reddish teak treated to a water-resistant coating by Brooks Custom. The Richard Mulligan stools were cushioned in Shelley Green cotton-viscose from Cowtan & Tout. The apron-front sink and the Waterworks faucets reiterate the traditional detailing of the millwork.

RIGHT, CLOCKWISE FROM TOP LEFT In the kitchen, polished-nickel hardware adds a hint of glamour and shine without looking too precious; countertops of white statuary marble have wraparound edges to create the illusion of a thick stone slab; iridescent, molten recycled-glass tiles from Walker Zanger in a thin, elongated shape create a sense of movement on the backsplash; the glass fruit bowl by artist Elizabeth Lyons was custom-colored to match the green stripe of the windowpane upholstery covering the breakfast-table armchairs.

RUGS AND CARPETS

One thing I especially love shopping for is carpets. A number of special ones enliven this house, including a Shaker-style braided area rug, hand-made in Pennsylvania, in the girls' hallway. We also ordered custom needlepoint carpets for the entryway and its adjacent powder room. Designer Ann Brandow of Vermilion has her rugs stitched in Brazil in any size and color. Her rugs in the foyer pick up the hues of the cream wainscot and the blue-striped hallway wallpaper to bring the decor down to the floor, where the pale shades contrast nicely against the dark walnut floors. In general, the bigger the room, the subtler the pattern. You can get away with a bit more visual interest in smaller spaces. For example, because the library is quite petite and also paneled entirely in wood, I didn't have to worry about a lot of competing color or fabrics and was free to play a bit with the floor, which I covered in a blue geometric-print rug. I have loved bold stripes since I bought my first Ralph Lauren rugby shirt in high school. A client once said to me, "No more stripes!" And I kept trying to sneak them in! Versatile stripes can be dressy or casual, and they allow you to bring multiple colors into a room, within a very clean composition. [S]

CLOCKWISE FROM TOP LEFT In the family room, the club chair fabric from Kravet has stylized flowers in strict rows, a parallel to the stripes of the Patterson, Flynn & Martin carpet; the foyer has custom needlepoint rugs hand-made by Vermilion (available through John Rosselli); a subtle plaid by Sacco Carpets, accented with chocolate brown, picks up the upholstery of a club chair; and in the library, the wing chair's rigorous chalk stripe by Holland & Sherry plays off a Sacco geometric-patterned flat-weave rug.

OPPOSITE The cheerful striped rugs in an upstairs hallway are from Patterson, Flynn & Martin.

THE GUEST-WING HALL

We nicknamed the little nook outside the laundry room "Key West." The space is very Floridian, with cream-and-lime-green wicker—and sunshine all day long. The "room," which I converted into a fully functional space, is actually a dormered hallway connecting the guest wing and the girls' bedrooms. It gives Samantha a cozy retreat to relax in while doing laundry; there's even a small flat-screen television recessed into the wall. Because the space is so snug, I chose only a single upholstery fabric: a leaf print in turquoise, green, and yellow. The chairs needed to be upright, to save space, but also comfortable. Wicker chairs proved to be the perfect solution because they are lightweight and easy to move. We spent a lot of time working on the design of the laundry room. The running joke was that since Dan got to have the Man Room, Samantha got to have a lady's room—a fancy laundry! I knew the door would always be open, so I thought the design should be fun and bright. Striped wallpaper and colored penny tiles conveyed the desired cheeriness. I agonized over the cabinet color, ultimately choosing white to match the woodwork. The laundry room has been luxuriously outfitted with a double set of full-size Miele laundry machines. ⑤

ABOVE LEFT Cream walls are offset by pops of color like the lime green tape that trims the wool carpeting from Patterson, Flynn & Martin.

ABOVE Colorful glazed penny tiles from Waterworks animate the floor of the windowless laundry room, which is equipped with two sets of Miele washers and dryers. The green-striped wallpaper is from Stark.

OPPOSITE Joining a grass green table from Maine Cottage is a custom-colored wicker armchair that transforms a hallway into a relaxing sunroom. Since the walls are painted cream, color had to come from the furniture as well as from the fabric, a bright leaf-print cotton by Osborne & Little. *Never Trust a Hippie* (2000), a silkscreen on paper, is by Scott King.

NEVER
trust
a
HIPPIE

A CHARMING GUEST ROOM

In a small room, it's nice to have just one or two fabrics. Toile de Jouy is a wonderful alternative to florals, especially if you prefer subtle, graphic patterns. I find the imagery and motifs of toile de Jouy to be more interesting and charming than those of floral patterns. The pattern always features bucolic scenes that give the fabric a real sense of narrative and history. It's fun and whimsical but still luxurious. S

OPPOSITE The bureau is one of only a handful of furnishings that the Andersons brought from their former house. The lamp is from Ralph Lauren.

ABOVE A golden toile de Jouy cotton covers the guest room walls, windows, lamp shades, and pillow shams. The pattern, by Laura Ashley (through Kravet), features pastoral scenes of maidens picking berries and sheep grazing. The bed is from Williams-Sonoma Home. Wooden shutters that block views while still admitting light are a great solution.

TOILE DE JOUY

Although *toile* means "cloth" in French, the term is used to denote a particular kind of textile: crisp cottons screen-printed with narrative scenes. When the fabric originated in seventeenth-century India, the whimsical imagery was painted by hand. As toile spread across Europe via trade routes, its popularity ultimately led to embargoes; France, for one, banned import and production of cotton from 1686 to 1759. The year after the ban was lifted, Christophe-Philippe Oberkampf founded a toile factory in the French village of Jouy-en-Josas (hence "toile de Jouy"), which Louis XVI soon designated as the royal manufacturer. At first, Oberkampf's designs were block printed, which limited the size of the repeats. Soon, however, the factory embraced copperplate engraving capable of producing more-intricate patterns, though only in mono-chrome, with drawings of the countryside or mythological events.

THE GIRLS' WING

At nine thousand square feet, the house is large, yet all the rooms are wonderfully scaled and rather intimate—including the girls' bedrooms. Samantha let her daughters choose their color schemes: Julia wanted pink, and her younger sister, Alexandra, opted for purple. I selected an assortment of fabrics, and the girls picked their favorites. Although both bedrooms have a youthful sensibility, the whimsical quality is tempered by all-white furniture and more sedate prints and stripes. The look is fun but not childish. The girls also have a shared play area nearby: the upstairs portion of the "knuckle." We could have just lined the hallway with closets, but the architect had the idea to transform it into a functional space. Built-in bookcases, storage, and window seats define a reading nook where Julia and Alexandra keep all their books, displaying them on the lower shelf like in a real library. The girls can pile up pillows and stuffed animals and snuggle into the window seat for a read. It's the perfect scale for kids, who like to take ownership of smaller spaces. ⑤

OPPOSITE The second floor of the knuckle hallway is a book nook for Julia and Alexandra. The window-seat cushions are upholstered in blue corduroy from SeaCloth and have crisp green piping. Braided rugs by Sacco Carpets lend a Pennsylvania Dutch flair.

ABOVE RIGHT The purple paint Alexandra chose was paired with lavender-and-blue floral draperies made from Cowtan & Tout fabric. The duvet and European sham were custom-made.

RIGHT Pink stripes perk up the draperies and carpet in Julia's bedroom. All-white furniture from Restoration Hardware tones down the bright colors and matches the woodwork of the girls' book nook. The tall headboard of the sleigh bed is comfortable for reading in bed. "I opted against a footboard, as it tends to cut a room in two," says Scott.

THE MASTER BEDROOM

I found a gorgeous lavender fabric for one of the guest rooms, but Samantha and Dan fell in love with it and earmarked the color scheme for their master bedroom instead. Walls painted in cream bestow a restful elegance and pair beautifully with the toile de Jouy used for window treatments, throw pillows, and shams. Although the color scheme still relates to the blue palette used throughout the house, the mood of the master suite is quite different from the other rooms—the atmosphere is especially relaxing and serene. The furnishings are also a little more formal and transitional here: polished finishes, a dainty desk with faux-bamboo legs, mahogany nightstands, and a beautifully delicate armchair with a lavender velvet cushion and hand-painted flowers along the top edge to match the toile. [s]

LEFT A windowpane-check Roman shade is coupled with pinch-pleated draperies in a muted toile de Jouy from Hinson. The draperies are lined to block the early-morning sun. Near a mahogany side table stands a club chair upholstered in a fresh silk stripe.

RIGHT A standard-height headboard works best in a room with a relatively low ceiling; the Andersons' master bedroom soars just eight feet. A Rose Tarlow Melrose House mahogany nightstand with open shelves keeps books and bedside essentials within easy reach. A Sheridan-style chair features hand-painted flowers that match the toile de Jouy fabric. "The hand-painting is an exquisite detail that would be less noticeable in a larger room," Scott says. A crystal lamp from Vaughan brings a note of luxury. "Pleated shades from the Oriental Lamp Shade Company add softness and romance."

CUSTOM BED LINENS

The fabric of the bed skirt and European shams should match the rest of room. My thinking is that if I'm already customizing a bed skirt and sham, then I might as well coordinate throw pillows and a duvet, too. So why not just do an entirely bespoke bed? Every bed has two sets of custom sheets. Guest rooms really need only one set each, unless you have frequent visitors. I like to mix high and low, pairing Frette or Ralph Lauren with Restoration Hardware, which sells well-made hotel-style sheets in many colors. I always suggest upgrading your everyday sheets because high-quality fabric will better withstand frequent washing. Pull the sheets out of the dryer when they are still slightly damp and then iron them. They'll last longer, and crisp sheets are so hospitable.

THE MASTER BATH

A lot of attention was devoted to the subtle detailing of the master bathroom. For instance, the shower is enclosed in glass to take advantage of the natural light and preserve the lofty expanse of space. But a glass shower smack in the middle of a room means having a view of all the fixtures as well. So to compose a pleasing pattern, we spent a lot of time sorting out the arrangement of the body sprays, showerheads, and handles. In addition to the double shower, there are his-and-hers vanities, a must in any dream home. As are both a shower and a soaking tub. The tub has the best view in the house, from a huge arched window overlooking the side garden. [s]

LEFT An expansive glass-enclosed double shower—with a pair of rainfall-style showerheads—preserves the room's open, airy feel while maximizing the influx of daylight. The subway and hexagonal mosaic tiles are fashioned from subtly veined marble. The fixtures are from Waterworks.

OPPOSITE A freestanding tub from Waterworks is positioned to take advantage of backyard views, including the formal rose garden. Shutters, used in place of draperies, withstand moisture well. "I particularly love them in a bathroom," says Scott. "The shutters offer the best of both worlds: They allow views out but not in, and the slats filter light beautifully. The look is very linear and clear."

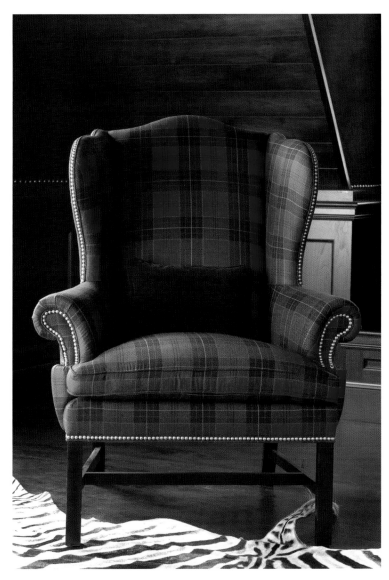

THE WING CHAIR

Every room should have what I call a "special" chair—one that lends a bit of visual interest courtesy of its profile but whose fabric ties the room together. A sofa or table wouldn't work as a "special" piece; it must be a chair! Most of the time, it's a wing chair, one of my signatures. A wing chair embodies the fresh, classic look I aspire to: The form is homey and inviting yet sophisticated. It's an understated statement piece and very

embracing: The high back and wraparound sides envelop the sitter, carving out a sense of intimacy and offering a perfect canvas for showing off a signature fabric. I often place a single wing chair in a corner, as I did in the living room. But I'll also group them in pairs, such as at either end of a dining room table. The Andersons have wing chairs all over their house—in the library, in the living room, and four very proud ones in the Man Room.

OPPOSITE A blue wool chalk stripe by Holland & Sherry brings gentlemanly flair to a wing chair from John Rosselli in the library—the room's only seat besides the desk chair.

ABOVE LEFT One of a pair of Ralph Lauren wing chairs in the Man Room is covered in a red wool Ralph Lauren plaid.

ABOVE Another wing chair has been treated to a navy corduroy from Holland & Sherry and nailhead trim that matches the detailing on the upholstered wall.

THE MAN ROOM

Dan was obsessed with having what he called a Man Room. I asked him what he planned to use it for, and he said, "Man things!" He just wanted it to be the most amazing space: drop-dead sleek and somewhat Ralph Lauren–inspired. So I designed it to look like a clubhouse, with seating areas suited to different activities: a tall table with stools near the wet bar, a game table for poker or backgammon, a television area with deep club chairs and corduroy-covered sofas, and—by the fire—a quartet of wing chairs on a zebra-skin rug. The colors are very masculine and deep; navy and burgundy fabrics offset the dark-stained woodwork. Although the architect had initially planned to panel just the inside of the dormers, once he saw the direction we were taking the interior design, I was able to persuade him to continue the black-walnut slatting all the way up the cupola to eliminate any trace of drywall. Rough-hewn walnut now envelops the entire ceiling, while the walls are swathed in navy felt with nailhead trim. Every surface is covered in a luxurious texture. The dramatic Man Room is a complete departure from the rest of the house. We were able to get away with it since the space is set apart from the other rooms. It overtakes the top floor of the barn, above the garage, and is hidden behind a giant wood door. Whenever Samantha and Dan give friends a tour of the house, the Man Room is always the last stop, and its paean to masculine style is always a surprise. [s]

OPPOSITE The quartet of wing chairs—two in red plaid wool, two in navy corduroy—create a formal seating group around the fireplace, where a graphic zebra skin softens the look of the chocolate brown floors.

RIGHT Furnishings in the Man Room hold their own against the dramatic architecture to create a clubby atmosphere. A replica of a 1920s wood speedboat from Yale R. Burge Antiques in New York sits on a console.

FAR LEFT The wet bar features Christopher Peacock Home cabinetry faced in nickel mesh and topped with dark gray soapstone. The glassware is from Baccarat, the vintage trophies are from English Country Antiques.

LEFT A replica of a 1964 Mustang Fastback mirrors Dan's full-size version, which dates from the following year and is parked in the house's three-car garage, under the Man Room.

BELOW, FAR LEFT A Richard Mulligan game table surrounded by Ralph Lauren leather armchairs adds to the clubhouse feeling. The padded navy blue felt walls are traced with nailheads to create a border.

BELOW LEFT Two different sizes of nailheads create a sharp, polished look along the arms and base of the Ralph Lauren corduroy-upholstered sofas.

OPPOSITE A jaunty plaid bedecks the draperies, pillows, and club chair seat cushions. Scott had the Sacco rug customized to match.

NAILHEADS

Nailhead trim is a versatile design accent whose effect depends on how and where it's used. The trim appears all over the house in various textures and sizes. In the Man Room, the nailhead trim works wonderfully; welting would have appeared too casual or preppy. The metal finish is quite graphic, accentuating curves in a bolder manner than a fabric trim. Besides a masculine touch, nailheads bring another texture to the Man Room: The shine balances out the rough wood and the navy blue felt walls. Otherwise, all those dark hues would have blended together, making the angled lines of the architecture indiscernible from afar.

Chapter Six
The Andersons at Home

Four years after meeting Dan and Samantha, their house was finally finished. Construction had wrapped, the interiors were composed and styled, and even the landscaping—always the last piece of the puzzle—was close to completion. All that was required to transform the house into a *home* was for the family to move in. The Andersons had asked me to be there when they returned from their vacation—a very flattering request. I drove over on a Saturday in April, about a half hour before they were due to arrive. I walked through the house, turning on all the lights and removing the blue-tape "velvet ropes"—the DO NOT ENTER signs we had hung on each of the completed rooms just the day before. It was dusk, and this otherworldly light suffused the space with a calming glow.

I had the house to myself for about twenty minutes before the family arrived. Everything was perfect, exactly the way I had envisioned it four years ago! I just sat and took it all in. This marked a very special moment for me—a brief sliver of time before turning over the project to the clients, when a house exists solely as a piece of art. I think painters must have this feeling in the studio when a canvas is finally completed, right before the gallery comes to pick it up for an exhibition. I had poured my heart and soul into this project, and it was wonderful to have some quiet alone-time to reflect on what it meant to me and to my career.

Then the Andersons burst in through the front door. It was just the most moving, fulfilling experience to see my wonderful clients take ownership of their dream home. §

LEFT This watercolor was painted by Scott when he was six years old.

PREVIOUS PAGES The three-and-a-half-acre property is stunningly landscaped and includes a formal rose garden surrounded by high hedges.

MEET THE FAMILY

As a designer, one always has a little flash of anticipation, and even nerves, when finally turning over a completed project to the clients. But Dan and Samantha were so present and involved in every aspect of the design that there was no way the house wasn't going to turn out perfectly. They communicated a very clear vision of what they aspired to. And they contributed to the process in such a positive, interested way from the beginning. To top it off, the three of us were completely in sync and had such a good rapport that it was easy to push one another to the best solutions. I would show Dan and Samantha an object or an accessory, and they would challenge me to find something a little more, say, clean-lined. Or I would push them to consider fabrics that were more youthful than they had envisioned. Earning that level of trust with a client is an amazing experience. It's what leads to the best design. As rewarding as it was to enjoy that solitary moment just before the Andersons moved in—when the house was purely a feat of design and not yet a home—it was even better to observe the space inhabited, to see the interiors as they were meant to be used, and to note how well the design supported their casual, easy-going lifestyle. The way the Andersons live is just how I grew up, too: wonderfully designed rooms, but nothing off-limits to children, guests, or Joey, their King Charles spaniel. The Andersons use every room, yet they still live elegantly. [s]

RIGHT The Andersons—Dan, far right, seven-year-old Julia, and Samantha with four-year-old Alexandra pose on the stairs of their new home.

"Together we dove into the design process with a passion to make the most unbelievable space," explains Dan. "We wanted the house to be elegant, comfortable, young, and vibrant—and to have an edge. Scott is an awesome listener and nailed our vision. He and his staff have a unique ability to respond quickly, which is critical for a client. There was a lot of back-and-forth, but we always came to a resolution in minutes. It was very much designed from the heart. I encouraged Scott to push the envelope—especially with accents and lighting—which excited him. We enjoyed a wonderful dialogue, trusting and valuing each other's input and opinions. When we returned from vacation and walked into our house—beautifully lit and with a bottle of champagne ready to go—I won't kid you: I had tears in my eyes. Samantha started crying the moment we stepped in the front door. We walked around the first floor, and I said to Scott with all sincerity, 'I don't deserve this! This is too nice.' We were just shell-shocked. Everything in the house was like eye candy: wow, wow, wow! It took a few days to finally feel that this was our house—that no one was going to come and take it away, so we'd better start enjoying it. And, boy, have we enjoyed it. Scott deserves so much recognition for everything he has accomplished. We really appreciate the value of what he contributes to a project—and the furniture and accessories he purchased on our behalf. I've said to him, 'Scott this is your house, too.'"

OPPOSITE Perched on the kitchen's teak center island, Julia enjoys a snack with her mother. The windows are framed with a valance that hides mesh roller shades that can be pulled down to cut morning glare. The stools are by Richard Mulligan; the lantern is from John Rosselli.

ABOVE RIGHT AND RIGHT Proof that it is possible to achieve an upscale, refined design that's also kid- and pet-friendly: Joey plays with the girls and Dan on the silk rug in the living room.

THE TEAM CELEBRATES

OPPOSITE AND RIGHT On the bluestone terrace, the Anderson family celebrates the completion of their new home by toasting those responsible for bringing it to life: architect Cyril Beveridge, in glasses and a bow tie; builder Mike Scheier, left and below left, with tan belt; designer Scott Sanders, in a blue-and-white gingham shirt; Scott's assistant, Jennifer Rock, in a navy top; project supervisor Ed Stern, in a pale blue shirt and jeans; and artist Sean Mellyn, serving champagne. For alfresco entertaining on the back terrace, food is served on white ceramic platters; flatware is wrapped in napkins and presented in tall plastic glasses; and melamine plates, dotted with butterflies, are as pretty as they are practical. The tabletop items came from home, james!, a shop in East Hampton, New York. The custom-made table, painted with white boat paint, is from Delgreco.

Moving On

One of the things I enjoy most about interior design is working on several projects at once. While one project may be nearing completion, the next could just be starting. All clients—their needs for the space, or their style—are also very different. But whatever their differences, there is a common thread tying together all the elements: classic furniture, clean lines, crisp fabrics, the use of color, and mixing antiques with new items. As I wrapped up work at the Anderson residence, I looked toward the future. A client I have worked with since starting my own company in 2000, who has a very traditional aesthetic, asked me to help her with the renovation of her modern beach house in Quogue, New York. My task was to bring the interiors more up-to-date and accommodate her family's love for music and entertaining. Another set of clients, whose loft-like apartment in New York I had decorated in 2005, decided to expand their space by purchasing the apartment next door. They hired me again, to design the new spaces to be multifunctional and kid-friendly yet sophisticated. A new library will not only be a quiet room for the children to read in but also a calm lounge where the parents can unwind from the day. I also just began a project with new clients in Tucson, Arizona—a beautiful 1920s Spanish-style house that is a vacation home now and will be a place for them to retire to later. While the couple does not have any children, they want the interiors to be comfortable, stylish, and easy for entertaining. My approach to design is always for the house to be a place to escape to, where one truly "feels at home," a place that reflects the family's taste through the layering of color, furnishings, and accessories. Our need for rooms that are multifunctional and approachable has increased over the years. Filling that request is one of the first things my clients ask of me. My rooms, which embody all these attributes, truly define the new American home. ⑤

SOURCES

This source list is a compilation of vendors who are my go-to people for every one of my projects. I believe in their products or services, have enjoyed working with them, many for over ten years, and have built not only professional but personal relationships with them. They stand behind their work or products and are dedicated to providing fine items for interior spaces.

ACCESSORIES & TABLETOP

Baccarat
625 Madison Avenue
New York, NY 10022
T: (212) 826-4100
www.baccarat.com

Decorum
248 Main Street
Amagansett, NY 11930
T: (631) 267-4040

Elizabeth Lyons Glass
More Fire Glass Studio
80 Rockwood Place
Rochester, NY 14610
T: (585) 242-0450
www.lyonsglass.com

home, james!
55 Main Street
East Hampton, NY 11937
T: (631) 324-2307
www.homejameseasthampton.com

Homenature
6 Main Street
Southampton, NY 11968
T: (631) 287-6277
www.homenature.com

Jarlath Mellett
255 Main Street
Amagansett, NY 11930
T: (631) 267-6455
www.jarlathdan.com

Lorin Marsh
The D & D Building
979 Third Avenue, Suite 720
New York, NY 10022
T: (212) 759-8700
www.lorinmarsh.com

Manhing Imports
240 Fifth Avenue
New York, NY 10001
T: (212) 684-5090
Fax: (212) 684-5091
manhing@msn.com

Mecox Southampton
257 County Road 39A
Southampton, NY 11968
T: (631) 287-5015
www.mecoxgardens.com

Ralph Lauren Home
T: (888) 475-7674
www.ralphlaurenhome.com

Ruby Beets
25 Washington Street
Sag Harbor, NY 11963
T: (631) 899-3275
www.rubybeets.com

ANTIQUES

Amy Perlin Antiques
306 East 61st Street
New York, NY 10065
T: (212) 593-5756
www.amyperlinantiques.com

English Country Antiques
26 Snake Hollow Road
Bridgehampton, NY 11932
T: (631) 537-0606
www.ecantiques.com

1stdibs
www.1stdibs.com

Huntting House Antiques
74 Montauk Highway
East Hampton, NY 11937
T: (631) 907-9616
www.hunttinghouseantiques.com

John Rosselli
Antiques & Decorations
The Interior Design Building
306 East 61st Street
Ground Floor
New York, NY 10065
T: (212) 750-0060
www.johnroselliantiques.com

Leo Design
413 Bleecker Street
New York, NY 10014
T: (212) 929-8466

Nellie's of Amagansett
230 Main Street
Amagansett, NY 11930
T: (631) 267-1000

Niall Smith Antiques
306 East 61st Street
Fifth Floor
New York, NY 10065
T: (212) 750-3985

Wyeth
315 Spring Street
New York, NY 10013
T: (212) 243-3661
www.wyethome.com

Yale R. Burge Antiques
315 East 62nd Street
New York, NY 10021
T: (212) 838-4005
www.yaleburge.com

ARCHITECTS

Beveridge Architects
Cyril Beveridge
534 Cokesbury Road
Annandale, NJ 08801
T: (908) 730-8836

James Paragano Architect
37 Kings Road
Madison, NJ 07940
T: (973) 765-0155
www.jamesparagano.com

ART CONSULTANTS

Mahony Dady Art Advisory
Maureen Mahony and
Jodi Dady, Principals
526 West 26th Street, Suite 805
New York, NY 10001
T: (212) 337-8071
www.mahonydadyartadvisory.com

Dr. Ruth Kaufmann
200 East End Avenue
New York, NY 10128
T: (212) 534-6148

ART GALLERIES

Jack Shainman Gallery
513 West 20th Street
New York, NY 10011
T: (212) 645-1701
www.jackshainman.com

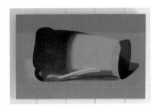

Jeff Bailey Gallery
511 West 25th Street, No. 207
New York, NY 10001
T: (212) 989-0156
www.baileygallery.com

Michael Steinberg Fine Art
T: (212) 924-5770
www.michaelsteinbergfineart.com

Pamela Williams Gallery
167 Main Street
Amagansett, NY 11930
www.pamelawilliamsgallery.com

303 Gallery
547 West 21st Street
New York, NY 10011
T: (212) 255-1121
www.303gallery.com

ART MOVERS

CFL Art Services
4325 38th Street
Long Island City, NY 11101
T: (718) 392-2500
www.cflartservices.net

BED LINENS

Frette
799 Madison Avenue
New York, NY 10021
T: (212) 988-5221
www.frette.com

Ralph Lauren Home
T: (888) 475-7674
www.ralphlaurenhome.com

Restoration Hardware
T: (800) 910-9836
www.restorationhardware.com

BOOKS ON DESIGN

Potterton Books
The D & D Building Lobby
979 Third Avenue
New York, NY 10022
T: (212) 644-2292
www.pottertonbooksusa.com

CARPETING & RUGS

Patterson, Flynn & Martin
(Division of F. Schumacher)
The D & D Building
979 Third Avenue
New York, NY 10022
T: (212) 688-7700
www.pattersonflynnandmartin.com

Sacco Carpet Corporation
520 Broadway, Sixth Floor
New York, NY 10012
T: (212) 226-4344
www.saccocarpet.com

Stark Carpet Corporation
The D & D Building
979 Third Avenue, Suite 1102
New York, NY 10022
T: (212) 752-9000
www.starkcarpet.com

Vermilion
(Exclusively at John Rosselli
& Associates to the trade)
The D & D Building
979 Third Avenue, Suite 1800
New York, NY 10022
T: (212) 593-2060
www.johnrosselliassociates.com

CATALOGS & WEB SITES

Crate & Barrel
T: (800) 996-9960
www.crateandbarrel.com

Pottery Barn
T: (888)-779-5176
www.potterybarn.com

Restoration Hardware
T: (800) 910-9836
www.restorationhardware.com

Williams-Sonoma Home
T: (888) 922-4108
www.wshome.com

CHILDREN'S FURNITURE

Maine Cottage
P.O. Box 935
Yarmouth, ME 04096
T: (207) 846-1430
www.mainecottage.com

Pottery Barn Kids
T: (800) 993-4923
www.potterybarnkids.com

CONTRACTORS

Custom Associates
153 West 27th Street
Suite 902
New York, NY 10001
T: (212) 242-3567

Michael G. Scheier
Scheier Building
6 Scarlet Oak Road
Califon, NJ 07830
T: (908) 439-1820

Scandic Builders
P.O. Box 411
Basking Ridge, NJ 07920
T: (973) 425-1228
www.scandicbuilders.com

CUSTOM FURNISHINGS & BUILT-INS

Antworks
168 North 14th Street
Brooklyn, NY 11211
T: (917) 304-5683
www.antworkswood.com

The Craftsmen of New York
Bob Livingston
347 West 39th Street
New York, NY 10018
T: (212) 947-0430

ELECTRICIANS

Custom Electric Design
Dan Mastroianni, President
P.O. Box 4205
Warren, NJ 07059
T: (908) 769-1490
www.customelectricdesign.com

Gabriel Velasquez
94-49 50th Avenue
Elmhurst, NY 11373
T: (718) 699-6333

FABRICS & WALL COVERINGS

Brunschwig & Fils
The D & D Building
979 Third Avenue
New York, NY 10022
T: (212) 838-7878
www.brunschwig.com

Cowtan & Tout
The D & D Building
979 Third Avenue, Suite 1022
New York, NY 10022
T: (212) 753-4488
Fax: (212) 593-1839
www.cowtan.com

Donghia
The D & D Building
979 Third Avenue
New York, NY 10022
T: (212) 935-3713
www.donghia.com

Hinson & Company
The D & D Building
979 Third Avenue
New York, NY 10022
T: (212) 688-5538
www.hinsonlighting.com

Holland & Sherry
330 East 59th Street
New York, NY 10022
T: (212) 758-1911
Fax: (212) 758-1967
www.hollandsherry.com

Kravet Furnishings / Lee Jofa / SeaCloth
The D & D Building
979 Third Avenue
New York, NY 10022
T: (212) 421-6363
www.kravet.com

Osborne & Little
The D & D Building
979 Third Avenue
New York, NY 10022
T: (212) 751-3333
www.osborneandlittle.com

Scalamandré
979 Third Avenue
New York, NY 10022
T: (212) 980-3888
www.scalamandre.com

Zoffany
The D & D Building
979 Third Avenue, Suite 409
New York, NY 10022
T (800) 395-8760
Fax: (212) 593-6184
www.zoffany.com

FAUX PAINTING

Tim Murphy Decorative Painting
306 Woolf Road
Milford, NJ 08848
T: (908) 996-0853
www.timmurphypaint.com

FURNITURE

David Iatesta
(Exclusively at John Rosselli & Associates to the trade)
The D & D Building
979 Third Avenue
New York, NY 10022
T: (212) 593-2060
www.johnrosselliassociates.com

Formations
(Represented by Holly Hunt)
8732 Melrose Avenue
Los Angeles, CA 90069
T: (310) 659-3062
www.formationsusa.com

Holly Hunt
The D & D Building
979 Third Avenue
New York, NY 10022
T: (212) 755-6555
www.hollyhunt.com

John Rosselli & Associates
(To the trade)
The D & D Building
979 Third Avenue
New York, NY 10022
T: (212) 593-2060
www.johnrosselliassociates.com

McGuire
200 Lexington Avenue
Suite 101
New York, NY 10016
T: (212) 689-1565
www.mcguirefurniture.com

O'Henry House
(Exclusively at John Rosselli & Associates to the trade)
The D & D Building
979 Third Avenue
New York, NY 10022
T: (212) 593-2060
www.johnrosselliassociates.com

Ralph Lauren to the Trade
Ralph Lauren Home
T: (888) 475-7674
www.ralphlaurenhome.com
All trade inquiries:
T: (212) 583-2200
www.rlhome.polo.com

Richard Mulligan
8157 Sunset Boulevard
Los Angeles, CA 90046
T: (323) 732-6380
www.richardmulligan.com

Rose Tarlow Melrose House
(Represented by Holly Hunt)
8454 Melrose Place
Los Angeles, CA 90069
T: (323) 651-2202
www.rosetarlow.com

KITCHENS & CABINETRY

Christopher Peacock Home
2 Dearfield Drive
Greenwich, CT 06830
T: (203) 892-9333
www.peacockcabinetry.com

Harmony Woodworking
153 West 27th Street
Room 902
New York, NY 10001
T: (212) 366-7221
harmonywwl@verizon.net

LIGHTING & LAMP SHADES

Architrove
74 Montauk Highway
East Hampton, NY 11937
T: (631) 329-2229
www.architrove.com

Carlos de La Puente Antiques
209 East 59th Street
241 East 60th Street
New York, NY 10022
T: (212) 751-4228
www.delapuenteantiques.com

Circa Lighting
405 Whitaker Street
Savannah, GA 31401
T: (877) 762-1008
www.circalighting.com

Kenneth Nilson
502 8th Street
Brooklyn, NY 11215
T: (718) 499-3884
www.kennethnilson.com

**The Oriental
Lamp Shade Company**
816 Lexington Avenue
New York, NY 10065
T: (212) 832-8190
www.orientallampshade.com

Paul Ferrante
(Exclusively at John Rosselli &
Associates to the trade)
The D & D Building
979 Third Avenue, Suite 1800
New York, NY 10022
T: (212) 593-2060
www.johnrosselliassociates.com

Remains Lighting
130 West 28th Street
New York, NY 10001
T: (212) 675-8051
www.remains.com

Vaughan Designs
The D & D Building
979 Third Avenue
Suite 1511
New York, NY 10022
T: (212) 319-7070
www.vaughandesigns.com

MESSENGER SERVICE

**BMW Messenger &
Trucking Service**
1270 Broadway
New York, NY 10001
T: (212) 889-2699

MOVERS

**S & S Warehousing and
Delivery Service**
57-10 49th Place Unit C
Maspeth, NY 11378
T: (718) 381-8300
www.snswarehouse.com

OUTDOOR FURNITURE

Delgreco & Company
The Fine Art Building
232 East 59th Street
New York, NY 10022
T: (212) 688-5310
www.delgrecoandcompany.com

Richard Schultz Design
The D & D Building
979 Third Avenue
New York, NY 10022
T: (212) 688-3620
www.richardshultz.com

Walters Wicker
The D & D Building
979 Third Avenue
New York, NY 10022
T: (212) 758-0472
www.walterswicker.com

PAINT

Benjamin Moore Paints
T: (800) 635-5147
www.benjaminmoore.com

Farrow & Ball
T: (888) 511-1121
www.farrow-ball.com

Pratt & Lambert
T: (800) 289-7728
www.prattandlambert.com

PAINTERS

WT Enterprises
Fine Interior Painting
William Tibbals
115 Perry Street
New York, NY 10014
T: (212) 463-7134

PICTURE FRAMING

Handmade Frames
526 West 26th Street
Room 212
New York, NY 10001
T: (212) 924-4316
www.handmadeframes.us

Skyframe Chelsea
141 West 28th Street
New York, NY 10012
T: (212) 925-7856
www.skyframeinc.com

REALTOR

Kate Tyree, Corcoran Group
1936 Montauk Highway
P.O. Box 3007
Bridgehampton, NY 11932
T: (631) 899-0322

TILE & TILE INSTALLERS

Chelsea Arts Tile + Stone
153 West 27th Street
New York, NY 10001
T: (646) 638-0444
www.chelseaartstileandstone.com

Michael J. Weber
Ceramic Tile & Stone
Installations
P.O. Box 159
Califon, NJ 07830
T: (908) 246-4043

Walker Zanger
37 East 20th Street
New York, NY 10003
T: (212) 844-3016
www.walkerzanger.com

Waterworks Operating Company
60 Backus Avenue
Danbury, CT 06810
T: (203) 546-6000
www.waterworks.com

UPHOLSTERY & DRAPERIES

Martin Albert Interiors
9 East 19th Street
New York, NY 10003
T: (212) 673-8000
www.martinalbert.com

WALLPAPER HANGER

BK Wallcovering
500 West 42nd Street
Suite 6B
New York, NY 10036
T: (212) 629-3040
www.bkwallcovering.com

I DEDICATE THIS BOOK

To my parents, Shirley and Charles, and to my grandparents Mimi (Mary) and Grandpa (Bill), for nurturing my creative desire to draw houses and design interiors as a child and for supporting my passion throughout my life. I cherish the love and dedication you have shown me.

To Dan, Samantha, Julia, and Alexandra Anderson: While your home is showcased at the end of this book, it is really how the book began. Thank you for opening your home and your lives to me and my office over the last four years. Our collaboration on every detail of the project and your willingness to allow me creative freedom is what has made this project such a success. It has been a pleasure to work with you, and I look forward to working together in the years to come.

To my boyfriend, Peter Wilson—my partner in life, my advisor, and my rock. Thank you for being in my life and for the love we share.

SPECIAL THANKS TO

My mother, Shirley, for saving all my house drawings, floor plans, and site plans from my childhood. Finding them has given me so much joy and has afforded me the opportunity to include them in this book.

Jean Wilson, my high school English teacher, for opening my eyes to a bigger world outside Piqua, Ohio.

Winston Miller, my manager at Ralph Lauren in New York, for believing in me and promoting me to be the first in-house interior designer at Ralph Lauren. Thank you for your continued support of my career over the years. I am so lucky to have you in my corner!

Mera and Jennifer Rubell, for giving me my first big design break. Their unwavering belief in my designs for their hotel, the Beach House Bal Harbour, was only the beginning of a long and wonderful relationship that I cherish. From Mera's providing my first design office space to Jennifer's many "home" projects and her invaluable advice, I feel blessed that I can call the Rubells dear friends.

Marjorie Kuhn and Caryn Zucker, for their continued support as both loyal clients and friends.

Roger and Bridget Ryan Berman and Jeff and Allison McKibben, for graciously allowing me to include their homes in this book.

Sean Mellyn, my best friend, for styling my life and my projects with his humor, creativity, and imagination.

Jennifer Rock, my senior design associate, for everything you do every day. Your devotion to your job and our office is admirable. You make everything work all the time, every day. You Rock!

Scott, photographed on a class trip to Chicago when he was eighteen years old, was then known as editor in chief prep.

Suzanne Slesin, fabulous publisher and wonderful friend, for making my dream come true. You are an absolute pleasure to work with.

Stafford Cliff, for capturing my life and career so dead-on.

Jane Creech, Regan Toews, Jonathan Lazzara, and Nick Santise, the team at Pointed Leaf Press: Thank you for making the process of creating this book almost effortless.

Michel Arnaud, for your incredible photographs of the Anderson residence. It has been a humbling experience to see my work through another artist's eyes, and it has been an absolute joy to have collaborated with you on this project. Thank you to your tireless assistant, Pawel Kaminski.

And also Joey DeLeo, William Geddes, Josh Klein, Michael Kleinberg, John Lei, Pat Miller, Marc Ricca, Patrik Rytikangas, Kim Sargent, and Jason Schmidt, for allowing me to include your amazing photographs in my book. It has been a pleasure to work with you over the years.

ACKNOWLEDGMENTS

Thank you also to the "Dream Team": Cyril Beveridge, Mike Scheier, Ed Stern, Arthur van Eck, Dan Mastroianni, Dan Minzner, Andrew Picone, Mike Weber, Edward Clark, and all the guys who were instrumental in producing the Anderson masterpiece. You created the beautiful foundation for my designs, and it has been an honor to work with such a talented crew.

Thank you to Jim Lyons and Shelley Selip at John Rosselli & Associates; Gary Levinson of Patterson, Flynn & Martin; Marc Sacco and Kim Steube of Sacco Carpet; Shirli Radziwell of Stark Carpet; Marc Issac of Martin Albert Interiors; the late David Zuch of Mark David Interiors; Margaret at English Country Antiques; Connie at Nellie's of Amagansett; Anthony Sisto; Tom Newman of Custom Associates; Ruth Kaufmann, Ph.D.; Daryl Bowman; Maureen Mahony; Victoria George; Garry Burrell; David Brogna; Alan Siegel; Orly Friedman; Kate Tyree of the Corcoran Group; and Mr. and Mrs. William Morris.

Thank you to Ingrid Abramovitch, Dominique Browning, Barbara Dixon, Stephen Drucker, Bernadette Murray, Lisa Newsom, Mayer Rus, Doretta Sperduto, and Newell Turner: We appreciate your recognition of our work in your publications.

Thank you to Tony Manning, Mary Lynch, and Kay Gilman of the Hampton and New Jersey Designer Showhouses.

To Ladye Kay Allen, Jane Benjamin, Travis Denton, Regina Seaton Oertle, Luis Perez, Maria Portera, Marianne Resman, and all my dear friends at Ralph Lauren: I began this journey with you by my side, and your support every step of the way has made it that much more enjoyable.

A heartfelt thank-you to my design associates, assistants, and interns over the years: Laura Carrigan, Leigh-Taylor Smith, Jennifer Jimenez, and Sheryl Danielian. The projects in this book would not have been a success without your hard work and dedication.

To all my wonderful clients: I cannot thank you enough for welcoming me and my office into your lives and allowing us to use your homes as our canvases. I would not be where I am today without you.

Scott Sanders LLC
27 West 24th Street
New York, NY 10010
T: (212) 343-8298
Fax: (212) 343-8299
www.scottsandersllc.com

My House Book By Scott Sanders HB

PHOTOGRAPH CREDITS

Unless noted below, all the photographs on location at the Anderson house, in architect Cyril Beveridge's office, and in designer Scott Sander's office were taken by Michel Arnaud between March and July 2009. The materials from the personal archives of Scott Sanders were photographed by Pawel Kaminski. Every effort has been made to locate copyright holders; any omission will be corrected in future printings.

Joseph De Leo Photography, 42–45, 56–59

William Geddes, 13, 48

House Beautiful, 39

J.Klein/JoshuaTreeStudio, 28–29

Michael Kleinberg, 30–31

© John Lei, 2009, 36–37

Joshua McHugh, 62, 63 (bottom), 67

Pat Miller Photography, 2210 Rte. 10, Muttontown,
    New York 11791, 34–35

Marco Ricca marcoriccaphotography.com
    (212) 529-2220, 38

Photograph by Jennifer Rock, 68

Photography by Patrik Rytikangas. 6, 32–33, 46–47,
    49–55, 60–61, 63 (top), 64–66

©2008 Kim Sargent, 69

Jason Schmidt/Trunk Archive, 40–41

Photo by Eric Striffler, 171

PUBLISHER'S ACKNOWLEDGMENTS

Suzanne Slesin and Jane Creech of Pointed Leaf Press would like to thank Dan and Samantha Anderson—as well as Julia and Alexandra—for their warmth and generosity and for allowing us to into their home even before they moved in themselves! Thank you also to Michel Arnaud, Stafford Cliff, Dominick Santise, Jen Renzi, and Liz Gall; and Stephen Drucker, David Friedlander, Pam Geiger, Pawel Kaminski, Jonathan Lazzara, Roger Ma, Sean Mellyn, Kathryn Millan, David Murphy, John Scott, Michael Steinberg, Eric Striffler, Regan Toews, and Newell Turner, who each in his or her own way made the creation of *Picture Perfect,* well, a perfect experience.

CAPTIONS

LEFT Scott's first book, self-published in 1969, includes many of his house drawings.

FRONT COVER A view of the finished Anderson living room is glimpsed through the foyer under construction.

ENDPAPERS FRONT A view of the living room fireplace is set among the fabric, wallpaper, and carpet samples used throughout the house.

OPPOSITE HALF TITLE AND ENDPAPERS VERSO An early formal front door drawn by Scott at ten years of age.

FRONT HALF TITLE A great moment, opening the door to the new house.

OPPOSITE TITLE PAGE AND TITLE PAGE The formal entrance of the Anderson house as seen finished and in the architect's drawing.

OPPOSITE CONTENTS Shelves in Scott Sanders' office present a tableau of vintage and contemporary cobalt glass including Elizabeth Lyons decanters and an English antique chinoiserie vase.

ENDPAPERS BACK One of Scott's subdivision drawings, complete with swimming pools, trees, tennis courts, several man-made ponds, and gates.

BACK COVER The living room is finally picture-perfect.

Pointed Leaf Press LLC
136 Baxter Street
New York, NY 10013
www.pointedleafpress.com

Printed and bound in China.

First edition
10 9 8 7 6 5 4 3 2 1
Library of Congress Control Number: 2009937623
ISBN 13: 978-0-9823585-1-1